A Promise
to Nadia

A true story of a British slave
in the Yemen

ZANA MUHSEN *with*

ANDREW CROFTS

SPHERE

First published in Great Britain in 2000 by Little, Brown and Company
This paperback edition published in 2010 by Sphere
Reprinted 2010, 2011, 2014

A CIP catalogue record for this book
is available from the British Library.

ISBN 978-0-7515-4369-8

Typeset in Centaur by M Rules
Printed and bound in Great Britain by
Clays Ltd, St Ives plc

Papers used by Sphere are from well-managed forests
and other responsible sources.

MIX
Paper from
responsible sources
FSC
www.fsc.org
FSC® C104740

Sphere
An imprint of
Little, Brown Book Group
100 Victoria Embankment
London EC4Y 0DY

An Hachette UK Company
www.hachette.co.uk

www.littlebrown.co.uk

Contents

Contents

Introduction

Introduction

I believe that two of the greatest struggles of modern civilisation have been the fights against the subjugation of women and the exploitation of children.

In Western countries huge strides have been made in both fields. Women are now legally entitled to equal opportunities in virtually all spheres of life. Children are now legally protected from exploitation by a host of laws and voluntary organisations.

Behind the closed doors of family homes, of course, it is not always the same story. There are still men who are willing to use their superior physical strength to dominate their partners and bully their children.

Sexual exploitation of children is the one crime by which everyone is morally horrified. Revelations still come to the surface of how widespread such exploitation is.

While First World countries continue to fight these battles, many Third World countries openly practise customs which amount to slavery for millions of women and children. The poorest people on earth can be bribed, with pitifully small payments, to sell their children into prostitution or into marriage, particularly if the children are girls.

It is still the custom in some countries for child brides to be sent to their husbands when the girls are as young as eleven or twelve. They are given no choice in this matter. They are simply handed over by their fathers to the fathers of their future husbands.

Most of these girls then go on to lead the life of a slave. They provide sexual services which endanger their health and they bear children for their husbands long before their bodies are ready. They work from morning to night to serve their men and the other elders of the communities in which they live, and they become old before their time.

They have no financial power and no way to escape from their fate. Legally, of course, they might be free to walk out of their homes whenever they wish. But where will they go? How will they eat? What will happen to their children?

Most of these women will stay with their children until they, too, are sold into marriage. By then, they themselves are too old and too tired to resist the exploitation of another generation of young people. (If you have worked like a slave for twenty or thirty years and your health is failing as a result, you are likely to be grateful when your son is married to an able-bodied young girl who can take over some of your duties and allow you to rest.)

The full horror of the lives which these people lead only comes to light in the West when a girl from a First World country finds herself enslaved in the Third World and manages to escape to tell her story.

In 1980, Zana and Nadia Muhsen, two girls from Birmingham in England, were tricked by their father into travelling to Yemen, where he sold them as child brides to two of his friends.

Zana escaped back to England eight years later, leaving her baby son behind. Before she left, she made a promise to her beloved sister Nadia that as soon as she reached England she would work to get Nadia and the children out.

Zana asked me to help her write a book called *Sold* about their experiences. The book was an international sensation, selling over two million copies. Tens of millions of people in Europe saw television programmes and read newspaper articles about the girls. The public outcry was colossal. Zana hoped the publicity which the book stirred up would mean that Nadia and the children would be brought home immediately. But Nadia didn't come home.

Nadia became as hopelessly trapped as any other Third World child bride.

In this book, *A Promise to Nadia*, Zana describes how she and her mother, Miriam, have continued the fight to free Nadia for the last ten years. It is a story which lays bare the truth about how a large proportion of the world's poorest women and children live.

She tells of their struggles with the Yemeni and British governments. She describes the succession of people who cheated her out of the fortune which she made from her book with their false promises of help.

While senior politicians continue to disclaim responsibility and the international community squabbles over whose responsibility Nadia should be, her life is ebbing away. Zana and Miriam continue to search for a way to reach Nadia before her health fails. The two women also hope to fulfil Zana's desire to see her son before he grows into a man.

A Promise to Nadia is a heart-breaking story of inefficiency and corruption, investigations, deception and theft that defies belief. It is a story of enormous courage and tenacity on the part of Zana, her mother and family as they battle to fulfil Zana's promise to Nadia, and it reveals the way in which women and children are still being enslaved every day.

It is a tale of hope and despair; hope that with people like Zana Muhsen fighting for justice things are bound to get better, and despair that anything will happen in time to save Nadia from her life of hell.

In the course of telling the story, Zana also tries to answer the questions of many thousands of people who have written to her after reading *Sold*, asking how she is managing to rebuild her own life in England.

Andrew Crofts
January 2000

I

Sold

I still wake up in the middle of the night, bathed in sweat and shaking with fear, having dreamed that, having gone back to Yemen to see Nadia ten years later, I am trapped once more.

It all still seems so real. I can feel the smallness of the room we are sitting in and the prying eyes of the villagers as they watch us. Some of them are silently suspicious and hostile. Others are shouting abuse at me for all the trouble I have caused them, all the shame which I have brought down upon them in the eyes of the world.

In my dreams they know how much we hate them and that we will do anything to escape. They know that we see them as our enemies and they are afraid of us, though they are the ones with all the power. They are able to dictate what will happen in our lives whilst we seem able to do no more than embarrass and temporarily inconvenience them.

But I am no longer as completely powerless as I was in the eight years that I lived there, either in my nightmares or in my waking life. I know now that I can fight and that I can win some battles. But no matter what I do, the Yemeni men are still in control. They are still able to threaten and abuse us and make us fear for our lives and the lives of our children. They can still do whatever they want to Nadia and there seems to be nothing we can do to stop them. They can sell our children, or make them work, or send them away.

Sometimes in the dreams I have taken my car with me – that treasured symbol of the freedom which I hold so dear – and I have managed to get Nadia and the children into it, along with some of my friends and relatives from England. It is a small car and we are all crushed in like sardines. We are so close our thunderous heartbeats are as one as we struggle to start the engine and make the machine move forward. The men are getting closer and I know that the car will be no protection unless I can get it to move quickly. They will overwhelm us, tip the car over and shake us out, like emptying coins from a child's money-box. We have to get away but there are too many of us for the little car and we are weighing it down.

In reality, of course, the suspension of my poor little Renault Clio would never survive the mountain tracks that lead to the villages of Mokbana. One sharp rock spinning up from our speeding wheels would have us out of action in no time. We would then be stranded in the desert, completely at their mercy once more. But these are dreams and so I am allowed to hold some hope that I can rescue my sister.

We are all jabbering in Arabic because we know that Nadia's kids can't speak much English. Our voices are high-pitched and panicky as each of us tries to be heard above the angry shouting of the men. In fact, the children's English is not too bad considering they have never been further from the village than the occasional visit to Taiz, but we are speaking in Arabic anyway.

All the men are armed, just as I remember them when journalists from the *Observer* came out to try to rescue us in 1987. Their fingers are on the triggers as they wave their weapons around threateningly. There is no doubt in my mind that they will use them. They would never have to face any legal consequences. Who would ever know if a few women and children disappeared in the mountains of Mokbana? People have been disappearing here since the beginning of time and no one on the outside ever knows what happens to them. The only thing that stops them from killing us is that they would then have no one to look after their children and homes for them; no one to carry the water or put their hands in the hot ovens; no one to carry firewood and plant their crops.

We can see the airport – as if we could ever get that close – but we never seem to be able to get to it. It hovers before us, a link with the outside world and people who will be kind to us and understanding, and it remains tantalisingly out of reach. We know that if we could just get there we could board a plane and our ordeal would be over.

But we never do get there. I wake up with a jolt, panting for breath. In the cold light of wakefulness it seems an impossible dream, and I feel clammy and sick with despair.

In our waking nightmares Nadia disappears for years at a time as far as we are concerned; during these periods we have no way of knowing if she is dead or alive. If we were told she

7

had died in childbirth or from malaria, we would never be able to prove otherwise. But in my dreams we are willing to take the risk of calling their bluff, because if we don't there is no other escape. Death would be preferable to spending the rest of our lives as their slaves.

Sometimes I dream I am staying with Nadia in her house in the village, and we are preparing for her to come home to England. I can smell all the smells and can feel the flies buzzing round our faces as if trying to drive us mad. She has no possessions which she wants to bring with her, but the children need to have certain things. The process of collecting everything seems to take for ever. I feel a rising sense of panic that the opportunity will pass and we will be told that we are not going. I urge her to hurry but she doesn't seem to hear, she just keeps moving at her own slow, steady pace.

Nadia's husband, Mohammed, sometimes comes into the room and apologises for everything he has done to her. We ignore him, not trusting ourselves to speak for fear that we will say something which will upset him and make him start shouting orders to stop us but we can't bring ourselves to actually tell him we forgive him, that would be too much. The time for apologies has long passed. The pain has gone on too long for forgiveness to be possible. We just want to be given the opportunity to forget at least some of the nightmare we have endured.

As I come back to consciousness from these night-time travels, I feel a wave of relief that I am safely in England, free and with my family. Then I remember that part of the nightmare is still real. My baby sister is still out there, growing old and sick at a speed which is unimaginable to anyone who has not witnessed it, and the misery returns. It fills my chest and knots my stomach and brings the tears back to my eyes. I know that at the same moment that I am lying there in my bed in Birmingham with Paul, my partner, sleeping peacefully beside me, one of the people I love most in the world is being slowly tortured to death. There seems to be nothing I can do about it. I feel hopeless and helpless and desperately sad, but my life has to go on.

I have my kids to wake up to and the routine of our lives to distract me. I am living in a free country. I can do pretty much whatever I want, except for one thing: I cannot see my sister, or talk to her, or know anything about what is going on in her life beyond the horrors which haunt my memory and my imagination. Despite everything that I have tried to do I still feel that I have failed her, because I promised to get her out and she is still there.

My imagination has plenty of material to feed on, because I once lived the same life. I endured the same hardships, the same bullying, the same monotony, the same gruelling work, the same ill health, the same neglect, the same rapes and beatings and humiliations. I know each time I wake up that another day has gone by in Nadia's life, another wasted day in which she should have been happy and free but wasn't.

I know that for another day I have been kept apart from my son, Marcus, and that I will never be able to recapture what we have both lost as a result. Another day of his life has gone by that I know nothing about. I don't know what he has done or what he has achieved. I haven't seen the changes that have happened to him nor have I been able to cuddle him when he was hurt or sick. I have no idea if anyone else has been filling my place in his life, since the day they said that I could leave but he must stay behind. No one has told me how he dealt with the shock of losing his mummy, the woman he clung to so tightly for the first two sickly years of his life. I have no idea what his personality is like now, or his health. I don't know what his voice sounds like or whether he laughs or cries most days.

Who wakes him up each morning? Who makes sure that he eats properly and that he goes to school clean? Who is making sure that he works hard so that he can get a decent job and escape from the drudgery of life in the village? I have no way of knowing and it breaks my heart. If his grandfather or father want to make him work like a slave or join the army or marry some girl in return for money, there is no one there to tell him that he doesn't have to do it, no one to explain to him that there is a free world outside the village and that he just has to find a way to reach it. He is a male child, and so he will have the power to escape eventually. But how much suffering will he have been put through before that happens? Will it turn him into one of them? Will he be as cruel and self-centred as his father and grandfather and all the other men he comes across in the Mokbana?

Not a day has gone by in the last ten years when I haven't cried. I think of Marcus and Nadia and I have to go off to a quiet place on my own so that the children won't see me upset. I want to get on with my life for their sake. There is no reason why they should ever have to know the things that I know. I don't want them to think back to their childhoods and remember that their mother was always weeping. Sometimes, however, they catch me out.

Cyan is only four. She has come across me crying once or twice. She has overheard enough conversations, understood enough snippets of television programmes, to have an idea that something is terribly wrong.

'I know why you are crying, Mummy,' she says. 'It's because of Grandad, isn't it? It's because he won't let Auntie Nadia come home.'

She has never met my father, but she has seen him on the television and she is petrified of him. She runs and hides as soon as his face comes on the screen. In her mind he has taken on the shape of a mythical bogey man who takes little girls away from their mothers, like a pantomime villain from some fairy story. There is nothing I can say to change the way she sees him. I could never, ever, let him get his hands on her for fear that he would do the same to her as he did to his own children. So there is no chance that he would ever be able to win her over and allay her fears. In truth, he is as bad and dangerous as she believes him to be in her childish imagination.

All I've told the kids is that they have an Auntie Nadia and lots of cousins in Yemen. I've explained briefly to Liam, the first child I had on my return to England, what happened to me and that he has an elder brother in Yemen, but he doesn't want to know any details.

I have explained to Liam that my dad sold me like a slave because I want him to understand the idea of slavery. I want all of them to understand the basics of the story as soon as they are able to absorb it, but I am careful not to scare them. One day they will know that they have a grandfather who says such dreadful things about black people like Paul and Jimmy (Liam's father), that he was once hauled before the Race Relations Board, but that time hasn't yet come.

For those who are coming upon my story for the first time, let me explain how it all began. I was fifteen and Nadia, my sister, was fourteen. We were as close as it is possible for two sisters to be. I loved Nadia like no one else. We understood each other completely and I always felt responsible for her. We lived in Birmingham with our mum and dad, our other two sisters, Tina and Ashia, and our little brother, Mo.

Dad was a Yemeni and as we became teenagers he started trying to bring us up in a strict, Muslim fashion. He didn't believe, for instance, that we should go out with boys or lead the sort of lives which all our other friends did. I was about to leave school and start training to be a nursery school teacher and I found his severe attitude annoying. But then most young girls find their parents annoying at that age. It didn't seem particularly unusual.

When Nadia was falsely accused of stealing a ring from a stall in the local market, Dad believed that all his predictions about how we would end up going to the bad had come true and he started plotting to 'save us' from the evil influence of the West. He asked us if we would like to go on holiday to the Yemen. He made it sound a very attractive proposition. In Yemen, we would have bare-back races across the desert and camel rides. We would build castles in the sand and all the rest. We both jumped at the offer.

I went out first, with Abdul Khada, a friend of my father's. Nadia was due to follow a couple of weeks later with Gowad, another friend. We had known both these men for many years and Mum trusted them to look after us.

It started as a grand, if rather frightening, adventure. It was my first time in an aeroplane, my first visit to a foreign land. The strangeness of the Arab culture and lifestyle was a shock – from the toilets and the food, to the heat and insects. It was all a new experience which I was keen to enjoy to the full. It was only after I had been there a few days that I discovered what had truly happened. My father had sold me as a bride for Abdul Khada's son, Abdullah, a thirteen-year-old boy so puny that he could never hope to catch a wife any other way.

Having lived my whole life in Birmingham as an English schoolchild, I suddenly found that I had become a Yemeni peasant woman. I was expected to serve the men of the family with complete obedience; to carry water on my head for miles each day; to cook, clean and provide sexual services to my 'husband'.

I was taken to my new family's village, Hockail, deep in the isolated, bandit-ridden mountains of the Mokbana region where there was no way for me to communicate with the out-side world; where all of the men carried guns and where nothing had changed for women in many centuries.

The worst part for me at the beginning was knowing that exactly the same fate awaited my beloved sister, Nadia, even though she wasn't yet fifteen. Her 'husband's' family lived in

Ashube, a neighbouring village about half an hour's walk away. His name was Mohammed and he was only thirteen.

To begin with, I had been sure that as soon as Mum realised we were not coming back after the two week holiday she would raise the alarm and the authorities would come and find us, but we had no way of knowing what might be happening in the outside world. What was actually happening was that Mum was going mad trying to find out where we were and Dad was refusing to tell her. The authorities were basically saying that there was nothing they could do about it as we were dual-nationals and we were now married anyway.

My mother is not particularly strong, either physically or emotionally, but she has the most extraordinary amount of will power. Despite the fact that she had endured two nervous breakdowns due to the way my father had treated her in the past, she absolutely refused to do what he wanted. He wanted her to shut up and accept the inevitable, but she just kept on banging on doors trying to find out what had happened to her daughters. She wrote letters, made phone calls and went to see everyone she could think of, but no one could help.

After six years, I managed to smuggle a letter out to her and she knew where to come looking. She had been involved in a motoring hit-and-run and received some compensation money which she used to pay for the trip. It took incredible guts for her to set off into such a hostile environment, one in which she could easily have disappeared, with no one in England any the wiser.

Nadia and I thought that as soon as she came she would be able to take us back with her, but it was not that simple. First she had to tell the British media what was happening and the *Observer* sent out a journalist and photographer to confirm her story. Nadia and I thought that they would be taking us back with them, but, just like Mum, they had to leave us behind. They promised that they would get us out as soon as they could. We knew that they had put themselves in considerable danger coming to find us, but we still felt let down to see them go.

It took two years of battling with the Yemeni authorities before I was allowed to leave the country. Eventually I was told that I could only go if I was willing to leave my little son, Marcus, behind.

Marcus is a teenager now, but I have not seen him since the day I flew out of his life, promising Nadia that I would do everything I could to free her and the children too. She had two children at the time, one of them was a girl called Tina and she couldn't bear the thought of leaving her behind. We both know the fate that lies in store for all young girls in that society. Nadia couldn't bring herself to desert Tina to face her fate alone.

I must have inherited a lot of Mum's determination. I have always felt personally responsible for Nadia and for everything that has happened to her. I was completely determined to get her out, even if it took me years to do it. I had no idea just how hard it was going to be. I had no idea how many people would stand in our way or the lengths that these people would go to in order to cheat and lie to us. I imagined that once I got back to the West and explained what had happened to us, the British government would insist that Nadia and the children follow. It might take a few weeks to arrange, or even months knowing how slowly things happened in Yemen, but it would happen.

At first, we could remain in touch with Nadia because she was still in the city of Taiz, but then she disappeared into the mountains and we couldn't make contact. She seemed to have vanished off the face of the earth. My sister had run through our fingers like sand. I felt overcome with guilt at being free while she was still imprisoned and I despaired of ever being able to find her again.

After a year of readjusting myself to life in the West, and of trying every official channel possible to get Nadia and the children out, I decided to write a book. I contacted Andrew Crofts and we created *Sold*. Reliving the horrors of those years was almost unbearable, but I was going to have to do it many more times in the coming years. I was prepared to go over my story again and again and again in the hope that eventually I would tell it to someone who would be able to help.

The literary agent who was trying to sell the book for us had trouble interesting a British publisher in the story. Everyone remembered reading about us in the *Observer*, but no one seemed to think that we had enough of a story to merit a full-length book. The *Observer* journalist who helped to get us out had also written an account of the story and publishers felt the public would not be interested in hearing any more.

Eventually, however, our agent managed to sell it for a reasonable amount but it didn't look as if the publisher was going to be able to promote the story much when it came out. We weren't able to give as many interviews as we would have liked because Mum and I had started a court case against Dad, Gowad and Abdul Khada. We feared we might prejudice the case and the whole project looked as if it might fizzle out. On top of that, the publishers were owned by Robert Maxwell and when he died the company went up for sale. No one had much time to think about a little paperback called *Sold*.

The agent then passed the manuscript on to associates in other countries and everything started to change. First a German publisher flew to London specially to meet us and made a generous offer for the German rights. Then the French came on board with a similar offer. Once the ball had started rolling, the offers just kept coming. Within a few months we had been signed up by publishers from as far away as Sweden, Denmark, Israel and Turkey. Film producers bought the rights to turn *Sold* into a movie, and a few years later it was even made into a radio play by the BBC for broadcast on Radio Four.

All of the foreign publishers wanted me to come to their countries and promote the book's publication, with press interviews and television appearances. They all did brilliant jobs. In fact, they did so well that the new owners of the British publishers – who were now free of legal restrictions because we had dropped our case against Dad and the others – decided to republish it in hardback with a new cover carrying a heartbreaking picture of Nadia's eyes looking out from behind a veil.

The French, however, were the ones who really took our story to their hearts, turning it into the best-selling book of the year in France in 1992. The public outcry over there was enormous. No one seemed able to believe that such a scandal could happen in the modern world.

Since then we have spent many years sitting beside silent telephones waiting for calls that never come. We don't want to push anyone who we believe is doing their best.

It's not that people don't care or aren't moved by our plight. A man called Pierre who lives in Canada started a website for Nadia. He asked people to send in their names and addresses. For each one he put a candle on the screen. Thousands of people responded. Now Pierre is using the information to petition the British and Yemeni governments.

Everyone we come across is always eager to help in the beginning – or at least they seem to be – and then something goes wrong. The government departments, the newspaper journalists, the charity workers, the book publishers, the film makers and the professional rescuers all find our story incredible when we tell it for the first time. More often than not they cry. No doubt they can picture the tragedy striking them or their children and they can imagine just how it would feel.

They are all shocked that such things can still happen in this day and age and they assure us that they can find a way out of the situation. They are outraged and angry. Sometimes they tell us that they just want to go over and get Nadia and the children back – killing anyone who stands in their way with their bare hands.

We leave these initial meetings with our hopes flying sky-high. We believe that this time we have truly found someone who will get something done. We go home and wait to hear from them.

Eventually we can stand the tension no longer and we ring to find out what might be happening. Slowly it becomes apparent that all their good intentions have been hijacked by other forces. Most of them just give up in the face of all the lies and bureaucracy. Some have made false promises and then stolen our money. Some seem to let other people persuade them that we are a hopeless case, that we are obsessed with freeing Nadia when really we should be giving up and leaving her alone.

It is impossible for us to understand how things have been allowed to reach this impasse. We are law-abiding citizens but we just aren't able to get anyone to help us right a wrong – one that is obvious to us and to the general public who read about us in books and in the newspapers.

Other people, who are initially shocked when they first hear our story, gradually accept Nadia's situation and are eventually able to put it out of their minds, when they realise how difficult it is going to be to help us. They have their own lives to lead, their own worries to preoccupy them. There are other deserving cases they can help out where they can be more sure they will get a result. But however much I might try to block it out, I can't help imagining Nadia's life out in Mokbana.

We have heard that she has six children now. It may be more by the time you read this. We know she walks with a limp because we've seen it in brief meetings and on the snatches of film that have got through to us. We don't know why. We don't know what has been done to her. We often imagine the worst.

I first noticed the limp when we went out to an arranged meeting with French camera crews but I blocked it from my mind. Later, Mum mentioned it to me. I wish she had never noticed it because she hasn't been able to get it out of her mind throughout the years.

Nadia has white patches of pigmentation on her skin, which looks dried up and sags from her bony arms and hands and sunken face. She looks tired and weak, so different to the beautiful, bright-eyed young girl who first went out there in 1980, different even from the sad-eyed young woman whose photographs touched so many millions of people when our story first broke in the *Observer* in 1987. But I know that whatever changes there may have been on the outside, she's still my kid sister on the inside, the high-spirited tomboy who was game for anything and who was always laughing. Behind the blank-eyed stare are the bits of her which she has buried beneath the despair and forgotten in the years of drudgery, pain and unhappiness.

I can tell, just by looking at photographs of her frail frame and haunted face, what she must be thinking. I remember thinking it myself; that I would die out there, be wrapped in a piece of white cloth and buried in the dirty ground with no one I really cared about ever knowing the difference. The men of the village would gather around the hole in the ground while the women watched from the distance and shook their heads in resigned sadness. The men would redistribute the little children amongst other female relatives and would go on about their business. Mum might never find out, though the chances were that my father or one of his friends would be unable to resist the temptation to taunt her with the news that one of her children was dead. Nadia must dread that happening just as much. Although perhaps the thought of death would be a release from the horrors of her daily life.

Every conversation Mum and I have about Nadia eventually comes back to Mum's worries about her health. Anyone who has had a child will know that no matter how old they are you always worry about them. If they are with you it's possible to nag them into seeing a doctor, going on and on at them until they are able to put your mind at rest. If they have made a bad marriage at least you are there to counsel them and provide some relief from the relationship and offer support should they decide to leave it. If you know that your daughter is being beaten by her partner, you can always make room for her in your own house, but Mum doesn't have that option. She sometimes has to go years without speaking to Nadia. Her imagination starts to work and she pictures the worst possible scenarios.

We know that Nadia does not have any access to medical help. We have no idea if she is in pain. I assume that she has become immune to any pain she may have, because that is what happens when you have to live with it all the time, with no hope of any respite. Your mind blocks it out so that you can go on with living.

I remember the pain I suffered when I was out there, and how I pushed it aside and kept going. I was determined not to allow it to defeat me. I came to believe that it was a normal part of everyday life – and for women in the villages out there it is – which I guess is a sort of brain-washing. As long as Nadia says nothing about her problems, as long as she keeps silently serving the other members of the family, no one will think to take her to a doctor and ask for someone to help her.

I can remember how shocked I was by the primitive lifestyles of the women in the local villages of the Yemen. I know that the millions of people who have read my book, *Sold*, have been similarly affected. I know because they write to me. The letters arrive in every imaginable language from people who want to know what happened to Nadia and me after the end of the book. Some of the letters are long and filled with anger and outrage. Every one of them makes me cry.

One of the first I received came from Sicily, from a man who claimed that he was a member of the Mafia. He told me how shocked he was and how he intended to hire a private helicopter and fly to Yemen to save Nadia and the children. Most of the letters are more down to earth, ordinary people expressing their sympathy, asking what has happened to us since, asking if there is anything they can do to help, telling me about their own lives.

An old man wrote to me from South Africa. He told me that he was bedridden and went on to relate his whole life story. It was so emotional that every sentence brought tears to my eyes. He was talking to me as if we were old friends. He had read the book and felt that he knew me well enough to confide all his secrets to me. It was a beautiful letter and I was very touched.

About sixty per cent of the letters come from women. I guess they can understand more easily what it is like not to be free. They understand how it is possible to put on a brave face for the outside world when you are screaming for help inside.

I would like to be able to answer every one, and to say, 'Yes please, do whatever you can,' but I don't have the organisation or the time to do it. All the genuine anger and kindness which the letters demonstrate goes to waste because we don't have any way to co-ordinate it properly. Everyone is willing to shout in our defence but we have no way of bringing their voices together so that they will create a sound loud enough to be heard in the government buildings where the decisions are made. If only we could find a way to harness all the goodwill which we have been shown in order to achieve something concrete, we would have had Nadia home years ago.

I know from the tone of the letters that I am able to read that all assume everything has worked out. They assume that Nadia and the children are now back in England, and that we are together and our nightmare has ended. No one imagines that our ordeal could have grown worse than it was when I was a prisoner in the mountains of Mokbana.

How is it possible that, after so much publicity and so much public outrage, nothing has been achieved? How can a child who was kidnapped at the age of fourteen still be a prisoner nearly twenty years later, when the whole world is aware of her plight? How can such a horror story have happened in these 'enlightened' times?

In 1992, everything was changing so fast that I was sure we would soon be seeing Nadia and the children back in England. I felt sure that, even though it had taken several years longer than I had anticipated, I was going to be able to keep my word to Nadia and bring her home.

2

'Zana, Say Hello to Your Sister'

Fixot, the French publisher of *Sold*, had promised to heavily promote the book, which in France was called *Vendues!* They more than lived up to their promise. The great break-through came when I was invited to appear on a live chat show called *Sacrée Soirée*. It is one of the most popular programmes in France, hosted by a man called Jean-Pierre Foucault and watched by millions.

I was terribly nervous when they first told me about it. To be appearing live in front of an audience of millions, struggling to talk through interpreters and to understand what was going on around me, seemed almost overwhelmingly daunting. But everyone backstage was very friendly and encouraging and I felt quite comfortable as the moment approached.

There was always someone from the publishers on hand to help me out, and I had Mum with me. There were moments, as the pressure was mounting, when I just wanted to run straight back to England and hide in my bedroom, but I knew that I had to do it for Nadia. This was our big chance. If I could get the message across to an audience this big I was sure that we would be able to get things moving. My main worry was whether I would be able to put my case convincingly in the allotted time. It was such a long story and so full of complications.

Everyone could see how nervous I was and worked hard at reassuring me. They had given me my own dressing room with my name on the door. Inside were champagne and canapés and light bulbs all round the mirror, just like in the movies. I didn't expect any of this sort of star treatment and in some ways it made me feel uneasy and guilty. I didn't want people to think that I was on some sort of ego trip when Nadia was still in Yemen, unable to tell the story alongside me. But I could see that it meant they were taking the book seriously and that was good.

My nervousness began to build as I waited behind the scenes for them to call my name. The cameras were rolling, the music was playing, the audience were applauding and Jean-Pierre was confidently babbling away in French. I could hear my name being mentioned but I had no idea what was being said. Then I felt myself being propelled forward.

The lights were hot as I walked out and my legs felt wobbly at the thought that there were several million people watching from home, as well as the invited audience who were enthusiastically applauding me. The cameras swooped in on me and it was hard to see the faces in the crowd, which was a relief. I concentrated on Jean-Pierre as he welcomed me like a good host and made me comfortable on the sofa. He talked to me for a bit and I began to feel more at ease. I could sense that the audience were interested in what I had to say and they seemed sympathetic.

What I didn't realise was that the producers had also invited the press attaché from the Yemeni embassy in Paris, Abdul Amir Chawki, to appear. After Jean-Pierre settled me down, he asked me to trust him, and then announced that Chawki was coming on to put forth the other side of the story.

For a second, all my feelings of panic returned, but as Chawki came on they changed to feelings of fury. I was tempted to hit him the moment I saw him. Mum was sitting right behind me, glaring at Chawki as if she might kill him. The audience were already sounding angry which made me feel better. I knew that they were on our side and I was ready for a fight.

Chawki had all the swaggering confidence of the men I had had to deal with in Yemen, but now we weren't in Yemen. We were in a French television studio and he did not have the liberty to talk to me as if I were an idiot just because I am a woman. I felt my courage growing with the anger that was boiling up inside me.

'Mr Abdul Amir Chawki,' Jean Pierre was saying, 'can you answer this: is it possible for Zana's son, her sister and the children to come back to Britain? What is your position and your country's position?'

Chawki was all fake sincerity and ingratiating smiles. He was obviously expert in dealing with the press, but he had misjudged the mood in that studio. He had come thinking that he would easily dismiss our ordeal as a preposterous story. His confidence came across as ugly arrogance.

'It is a terrible and dramatic situation and I sympathise with Zana,' he said, patronisingly. 'It is a drama and it is her father's fault. A lot of time was wasted when they were hidden in that village in Yemen.'

Jean-Pierre interrupted, obviously irritated by Chawki's evasiveness. 'What can you do to help Zana and her sister as you find the situation unacceptable?'

'I am very upset by this story.' Chawki put his hand on his heart as if it was about to break. 'I am a human being. My department and Yemen have done a lot to resolve things.'

That was too much for me. I wasn't going to sit and listen to any more of this nonsense. 'They should have worked on this twelve years ago!' I snapped. 'They knew, very well, what was wrong.'

'The government learned about it when it all came out,' Chawki continued smoothly as if I hadn't spoken. 'We tried to resolve the problem and immediately we put Zana and her sister under protection, to take them away from family pressure.'

They did put us under 'protection' for as long as they felt they had to, but who was protecting Nadia now? And was protection not just another word for imprisonment? We might have been removed from the hard labour of village life for a few weeks while they tried to sort out what was going to happen to us, but all it really meant was that we were prisoners of the government instead of prisoners of the families who had bought us from Dad. It was all political games and it made me want to scream with frustration.

Chawki, however, was hitting his stride. He stretched his

arm along the back of the sofa we were both sitting on, as if relaxing for an evening of gentle debate amongst friends. I shrank from him. I was reminded of every patronising gesture I had suffered at the hands of Abdul Khada and the other men. Jean-Pierre gave me a concerned look. He must have been worried that I might walk off the set if things became too much for me. I didn't realise it at the time but he had another dramatic surprise in store which he wouldn't have been able to spring if I had stormed off.

'Can Zana go back to Yemen freely and see her sister?' he asked Chawki directly.

Chawki didn't miss a beat. He was a professional. 'Zana was free from day one as she is a British citizen. Her mother went to Yemen twice to see the child and Zana could have gone there too.'

As if I would have dared to return to Yemen, after eight nightmare years, with the ever-present threat that I might be abducted and taken straight back to the village. I could just imagine the revenge which Abdul Khada would take on me for all the things I had written about his treatment of me in the book. To have gone back to Yemen unprotected would have been suicidal.

It seemed that Jean-Pierre, with his carefully considered words, was preparing to spring a trap on Chawki. 'If tomorrow, or the day after tomorrow, or even on Friday, I went with Zana – and obviously *Sacrée Soirée* – to Yemen, do you guarantee that we will be able to meet her sister and the children, so that, humanely speaking, all is resolved more quickly?' he asked.

'Officially speaking, there is no problem on our side,' Chawki said. He still hardly missed a beat. There was a thin film of perspiration on his skin, but his smug smile did not waver.

My head was spinning. This was the first I had heard about a plan to take me to Yemen. The thought of seeing Nadia and Marcus was wonderful, but at the same time I was terrified at the thought of going back to the place which haunted my nightmares. What if they grabbed me while I was there? What if they threw Jean-Pierre into jail and took me back to Mokbana? What if they arranged for a car crash, or a plane crash, or what if they just shot us in the street?

Jean-Pierre was speaking to the camera. I could hear his words but I wasn't taking them in. I was too busy trying to digest the last piece of news and work out what my response should be.

'Nadia is in Yemen and she has not spoken to her sister for four years,' Jean-Pierre announced.

'Four years ago,' I said, unable to stop the tears from coming to my eyes, 'she told me to get her out of there as soon as possible.' I was trying to clear my own thoughts as much as anything else. I needed to remind myself what the primary goal was. My priority had to be the promise I had made to Nadia. But since then I had had Liam. I had to consider him as well. I didn't want him to lose his mother when he most needed her, as Marcus had done.

'In Taiz,' Jean-Pierre said, 'Nadia is waiting on the telephone to speak with you, Zana. Say hello to your sister . . .'

The whole studio was as silent as a church. I was overwhelmed by confusion. I had been trying to sort out my thoughts and now they were telling me Nadia was waiting to speak to me? I couldn't believe it was true.

All I could hear was the roar and crackle of static as they broadcast the telephone line to Taiz over the loudspeakers. I could hear her voice but it was impossible to make out what she was saying. The tears poured down my cheeks unchecked as I imagined her at the other end of the line, trying to work out what was going on.

I knew she would be surrounded by men, all of them telling her what to say and what not to say. She would be as confused as I was, having been fetched, probably without explanation, and whisked to the telephone. She would know nothing about the book or the television programme or why she was suddenly being allowed to speak to me after so long. She would be straining to hear my words as much as I was straining to hear hers.

Jean-Pierre then announced that there would be a short break in the programme while I went to talk to Nadia from an office behind the scenes. I was still in a state of shock, but it was a relief to think that I would get away from the studio and the heat and noise for a few minutes. Mum came with me. I could see that she was as stunned as I was, both of us trying to make sense of things.

Dazed we walked off the set with Jean-Pierre as the music swelled up around us. A group of musicians filled in while we were off. It was odd to hear happy music when we were going through so much trauma. We couldn't take in everything that was happening, we just had to allow others to guide us to where they wanted us to be.

I was desperate to get to the phone before the line was cut. I could imagine how edgy the men would be in Taiz. They were probably at Nasser Saleh's house, the man who had acted as agent for Dad, Gowad and Abdul Khada. Nadia's husband, Mohammed, would be there, and probably several others. They would be arguing amongst themselves about the wisdom of what they were doing, and it was quite likely that they would decide to sever the connection without any warning to save any further embarrassment. They could always blame the bad telephone lines.

I was terrified that by the time I got to the phone there would be nothing but a dialling tone. It was such a fragile, tenuous link. It was as if Nadia was hanging over the side of a cliff, holding on to a piece of string. If the string snapped she would disappear for ever.

By the time we got to the office, where the phone was being held for me, I was crying too hard to talk and Mum took the receiver from Jean-Pierre. Mum started to cry now as well, her voice cracking as she spoke. I managed to compose myself, inhaling enough to have the breath to talk. All I could think of to say were the sort of banal pleasantries that I might have used if I had been speaking to her every day.

'How are you, Nard?' I asked.

'I've had another kid, Zane. I'm back living in the village.' Her Brummie accent hadn't changed. It was as if we were still back in Birmingham, when we were fourteen- and fifteen-year-old sisters discussing our personal lives.

'What?' I couldn't believe it. In my mind I had hoped that she was being looked after in Taiz and that she was waiting in the city for the plane to bring her back to England once everything was sorted out. I had imagined that the 'protection' from the authorities – which Chawki had talked about so proudly – had continued after I left. Now I realised that they had taken her back to the same life that she and I had endured before. I had escaped and she had not. The news that she had had another baby was shattering.

It meant that Mohammed was still able to demand his marital rights whenever he chose, and the thought of my baby sister being continually raped made me feel sick. Even worse was the knowledge that after she gave birth to Tina, her second child, the doctors had told her she should never have any more children. Now she had had two more in quick succession.

They were controlling her by keeping her pregnant. She was weighed down with children, with no time for herself and no time to think, argue or rebel. Gowad had bought her from Dad in order to produce grandchildren for him and she was going to have to meet that obligation until the day we managed to get her back to England or until she died or became too old.

I felt a ball of anger and frustration building up inside me once more. We had to get her out and we had to do it now, before they killed her with their insatiable demands on her already frail body.

I asked her a few more questions, and tried to find out what had happened to Marcus. She asked me what was going on in Europe. I tried to explain everything that had happened in the last four years but my words were falling over one another and then the line went dead. The string had been cut.

I knew she must be feeling even worse than I was. She was still in a room full of men in Taiz after a few minutes of being able to reach out to her family and home and hear friendly voices from her past. As I stood, holding the dead phone, I imagined how all the men would be shouting at her, telling her what she should have said and arguing amongst themselves about what they should do next, while she sat amongst them, probably not even able to muster tears in her blank, staring eyes.

I was struggling to straighten out my thoughts, and the floor manager was trying to shepherd us back on to the stage. The musicians were ending their number. The whole thing must have been over in a few minutes but I had no concept of time any more.

The next thing I knew, we were being brought back out into the hot spotlights and Jean-Pierre was greeting us. He wanted to know what had happened. I wasn't sure that I was going to be able to speak. To my relief, the words started to come.

'Nadia is back in the village,' I said, feeling as if every word was going to choke me. 'She has been there since just after I left Yemen. She has had another baby now.' I could hear my own voice and the words were as shocking to me now as they had been when Nadia first spoke them.

'And Marcus, what about him?' Jean-Pierre asked.

'He was taken from her just after I left the Yemen. She hasn't seen him since. He's gone. He's disappeared!' I thought I was going to lose control as I remembered the sad, skinny little infant I had left crying in Yemen the day I finally escaped. I held on as tightly as I could, shaking with anger and misery, wanting the whole ordeal to be over so that Mum and I could talk.

'What will you do now?' Jean-Pierre asked. 'Will you give up?'

'No!' The word came out with all the force of my soul. 'Never! I'm never going to give up. I want Nadia to come to England with the children and prove that she is free. I'll never give up until she comes home.'

'Thank you, Zana,' Jean-Pierre said. 'We wish you all the success in the world with your book and hope that Nadia will be free soon.'

The show was winding down and I could see my face on the monitors all round the studio – my eyes red and my cheeks wet with tears. The audience were clapping in time to the music. It was all over and I was left on the sofa feeling as if I had been hit by a ten-ton truck.

I kept my head up, determined not to let Chawki see any weakness in me. Mum put her face in her hands and the camera immediately turned on her. I leant across and pulled her hands away.

'Don't let them see you cry, Mum,' I said. 'Don't let them see you cry.'

As Mum tried to compose herself, Chawki smirked at her, and her grief turned to rage. She flew at him, grabbing him by the neck and screaming at him. 'You bastard. You lying Arab bastard!'

The cameras were switched off but the audience still applauded. They had seen the whole thing and they knew who was lying and who was telling the truth. They could see the same smug expression on his face that we could see. He

35

represented those who still held Nadia and the children prisoner. We were no more than a minor irritation to him, no doubt, an opportunity for him to further his career in the diplomatic service.

Bernard Fixot, my French publisher, pulled Mum off and tried to calm her down. Chawki was led away, visibly shaken, as the audience booed and shouted insults at him. Then the audience started cheering us and chanting, 'Nadia libre, Nadia libre,' as we finally left the stage.

We had taken a giant step forward, we knew that. Now our story had been turned into a major news event. It had been given a spin and a gloss by the show business approach of *Sacrée Soirée* and we were deeply grateful – if a little shell-shocked. If this was what it took to get Nadia back, then we were more than willing to go through with it.

The millions who had witnessed the whole drama on their television screens had been as moved and as angered as the studio audience. Over the next few weeks they flooded the Yemeni embassy with letters. The newspapers also followed up the story, demanding that something should be done. The sad sisters of the Mokbana had become a national scandal. The public wanted to know more and to see a solution found.

When they realised what a sensation they had created, the producers at *Sacrée Soirée* wanted to follow through the huge groundswell of interest. Jean-Pierre asked me if I would be willing to appear on the programme again and whether I would be prepared to travel to Taiz with him and a camera crew the following day if Chawki could be forced to agree on the show to arrange it.

I had often thought about going back after that first show. Mum and I had talked about little else. Although I told myself that I would be protected by both the television people and the publishers, who I knew would be there, I knew that it was dangerous. My natural instincts warned me that I should never go near that country again.

But I also knew that we were on the crest of a wave. If we could keep up this international pressure we might be able to force the Yemenis to give in. We might be able to make it so embarrassing for them that they would rather lose face and hand over Nadia and the children than prolong the agony of being exposed on French television.

I told Jean-Pierre I would happily go on the show again, but I would have to think about whether I could face returning to Yemen.

The show was set up and Chawki was invited back. He now seemed a lot more nervous than we were. We had been told that the Yemeni Ambassador in Paris had been keen to let Nadia and the children out immediately to save any further embarrassment, but it seemed Chawki had persuaded him to do nothing. Chawki was willing to defend his position in public. He was prepared to gamble his career on being able to save the situation in some way. We were gambling everything on being able to outwit him.

He was full of more patronising statements and false assurances about how I was free to go to Yemen whenever I wanted. 'Of course' I could visit my family. I suppose he was confident that I would never have the courage to return. He could keep issuing meaningless invitations, making it look as if they were trying to solve the situation while I was being difficult and obstructive.

He kept repeating phrases like, 'Nadia is a Yemeni citizen,' and 'She is happy, she doesn't want to come out.'

'So, Zana,' Jean-Pierre turned to me. 'Do you accept to come with us, to Yemen? Tomorrow? To sort things out?'

I heard his words and I took a deep breath. The audience hardly seemed to breathe either as they waited for my reply. I looked at Chawki's smug face. He was waiting to crow over my lack of co-operation. It was like plucking up the courage to jump into a cold swimming pool. I took the plunge.

'Yes,' I said, 'I accept.' The audience applauded and Chawki looked suitably shocked for a few moments as he rethought his position.

'If you were in Zana's position,' Jean-Pierre said to him, 'would you have done everything to get this story out in the open, in front of the whole world?'

Chawki looked very uncomfortable. He began to sweat and tried to change the subject. 'Your dad's problem is dramatic,' he told me. 'The Yemeni government took away his passport from him.'

'It's not true,' I said. 'My dad had a British passport.'

'He still had a Yemeni passport,' Chawki mumbled, playing for time as he tried to think of something more convincing to say. The audience hissed their disapproval of his weasel words.

Jean-Pierre shook his head as if despairing. 'If we don't give enough publicity to this story, the problem will never be resolved,' he said. 'Zana, the author of *Vendues!*, will go to Yemen with *Sacrée Soirée*.'

Having made the decision, I was terrified. 'I don't want to do it,' I told Mum as soon as we were safely back in our hotel room.

'We've got to try, Zane. We've got to let Nadia know what's going on, that she's not on her own, that we're still fighting to get her out.'

There was no stopping the bandwagon now. Both the publishers and the television producers believed it was the only route forward and everyone started to negotiate the best way to arrange things. Mum and I were little more than pawns, being moved about in their great game of chess. We spent a lot of time waiting in hotel rooms, puffing nervously on cigarettes.

Every so often we would receive bulletins on how things were going. We were told that the Yemenis had agreed we would be able to see Nadia and the children for as long as we wanted, and that I would be able to see Marcus.

'And if you want to take Marcus out of the country,' Chawki said, 'you can make an application to the courts.'

I knew I shouldn't believe a single word of it, but when you are drowning you will clutch at anything and this thin promise made me feel optimistic. Everyone was so enthusiastic about it I couldn't help but be swept along with them, although the doubts kept nagging at the back of my mind and the fear kept stirring in the pit of my stomach.

Jean-Pierre knew I was frightened. 'Don't worry,' he said, 'if they try to kidnap you, I will be your ransom.'

I knew that he was trying to be comforting, and I knew that he meant it. I also knew that such gestures would be meaningless once we were in Yemen. If they decided to hold on to me there would be nothing that Jean-Pierre or Bernard Fixot or anyone else would be able to do about it. They could protest all they liked. They could write letters to heads of state and organise television programmes every day of the week, it would make no difference.

But if I wanted to get Nadia and the children out, it was a risk I was just going to have to take.

From the moment I agreed to go to Taiz everything became a confusing rush. Mum's passport had run out and she hadn't noticed. We couldn't risk going to Yemen with an out-of-date passport – we didn't want to give them any excuse for making it difficult for us to get in or out of the country – so we had to get it renewed in a hurry. We also had to get Yemeni visas from Chawki.

Yet again, he was in a position of power over us and he didn't hesitate to take advantage of it. We had to promise not to try to snatch Nadia or the children while we were there. Quite how he thought we would be able to do that, when we were in full public view, with an entourage of cameras, I don't know. I guess he just wanted to make the point that he didn't trust us any more than we trusted him. Of course he was right not to trust us. If I had been able to think of a way to kidnap Nadia and the children I would have done it, regardless of any promises I might have made to Chawki.

Bernard Fixot, my publisher in France, is a great cuddly bear of a man whom I had met on my first trip to Paris and who had cried openly when he heard my story. I think it was because of his personal interest that the book had been so heavily and successfully promoted.

His wife, Valérie-Anne, is also an influential figure in Paris, being the daughter of Valéry Giscard d'Estaing, the former President of France. Both of them were convinced that we had made a big step forward. They would be coming down to Yemen with us. Valérie-Anne had offered herself as surety that no snatch would be attempted if they would allow us to be alone with Nadia. Because of the importance of her father, Valérie-Anne's offer probably held more weight than Jean-Pierre's. It meant that Chawki could show his bosses how careful he was being and how high a price he was demanding for their co-operation.

Someone chartered a private, ten-seater plane and we all flew down to Taiz. Chawki took advantage of the free flight to visit his friends and family.

On the plane, Jean-Pierre could see that I was becoming increasingly nervous as I pictured the many things that were likely to go wrong once we got there. He asked if I was all right.

'I'm all right,' I said, though I knew my nerves were almost at snapping point. 'I'm telling you, though. I know these people. It won't go as planned. You can't plan anything in Yemen. They'll have the place crawling with government officials, and the army and police, too. They won't bring all the children. You watch. I'm not wrong. You wait and see!'

I hated being so pessimistic when they were buoyant and expecting the best, but I couldn't stop myself from voicing my doubts and fears. I knew I was being realistic. I was the only one in the party who had lived in Yemen – apart from Chawki – and I knew how things always went. I chain-smoked, gnawed viciously at my finger nails and imagined how Nadia was spending the day.

Assuming they had taken her back to the village after the phone call to the programme, she would have to have been brought back in a Land Rover. She would probably not have been told what was happening, just ordered to be ready to travel. Once she got to Taiz they would begin drilling her in what she should and should not say to us and to the cameras. They would want us to hear her say how happy she was, and how she didn't want to return to England. I prayed that she would realise how important it was that she didn't do as they said, but I knew that they would be going on and on at her. I knew they would hit her if she showed any sign of rebelling.

I tried to think of something other than the abuse. I tried to imagine that the children were with her. I couldn't picture what Marcus looked like after four years. I knew he wouldn't recognise me – and if he did he would probably hate me for leaving him when he was so tiny – but I still longed to be able to look at him and, hopefully, give him a cuddle. I wanted to be able to tell him that I hadn't deserted him, that I was working to get him free so that we could be together again.

When I left he had been too young to understand anything that was going on. Now he would at least be able to hear my explanation. At least he would know that he did have a mum and that she loved him, even though she couldn't be with him. I blinked back the tears and stared hard out of the window, hoping that no one else would try to talk to me.

They were warned by my expression and left me alone with my thoughts.

When we arrived at Sana'a airport my worst fears were realised. There were at least thirty official-looking men waiting for us, some of them armed and keen to let everyone see their guns. There was also a local film crew, hired no doubt to show the foreigners that the Yemeni media were also free to cover the story. I hated to think what the Yemeni public were being told about the case.

The officials took our passports and Chawki disappeared with his friends. He looked a great deal more comfortable now that he was back on his home territory. Here he was someone of importance and his power was very real.

As I looked around I could see that everyone was busy whispering and arguing, leaving Mum and me sitting alone. All my memories of the smells of the place and the sounds of Arab voices came back, making me tremble. The presence of Bernard, Valérie-Anne and Jean-Pierre, who were such confident, powerful people in Paris, suddenly seemed less reassuring. It was obvious that they weren't sure what was going on, any more than we were. We all waited until we were told what our next move would be.

Eventually we were flown on to Taiz. We arrived in the evening, and were checked into the Sheraton Hotel. We were told that the meeting would take place the following day.

Mum and I shared a room and sat up all night smoking and drinking tea, alternating between long silences and going over the same ground a hundred times as we stared out at the twinkling lights of the city. The hours dragged on for ever until we heard the wake-up calls from the mosques as the imams called the faithful to prayer and dawn broke slowly over the rooftops. The lights were turned out as the heat of the day began to build.

We were tense and exhausted and impatient to see Nadia and the children. The arrangements seemed to take hours. Eventually we were driven to the city centre.

On the way, officials told us that we would be able to meet Nadia in a private room and talk for as long as we wanted. My heart was beating in my ears and I found it hard to get my breath as the moment drew near. Every time the car slowed for a junction I expected someone to stop us and tell us that the whole thing had been cancelled, or that Nadia wasn't there and we would have to come back the next day, or the next week or the next month. I didn't dare to allow myself to believe that they were actually going to keep their word and let us see her immediately.

We arrived at a nondescript government building and we were shown into a garden at the back where we waited once again. There was a patio with three seats and a small table, surrounded on three sides by a high white-washed wall. The *Sacrée Soirée* team quietly set about arranging their cameras and lights. I still could not believe that it was actually going to happen, that I was actually going to be able to talk to her face to face after four years.

All around the garden, keeping a respectful distance, were thirty or forty Yemeni men, probably the same ones who had been waiting for us at the airport. Some of them had video cameras. More and more Land Rovers kept turning up and each time I expected to see Nadia get out, but it was always more men who strutted about looking important and issuing orders.

We sat in the garden for two hours, watching as these men wandered around with their guns, whispering to one another and glancing in our direction. It was as if they were deliberately trying to make us nervous and undermine our confidence. The tactic was working. Nevertheless, we were completely determined to outlast them. It was like a grotesque game of 'call my bluff'.

As we watched the number of arriving officials grow, Mum and I both realised we had made a mistake. We had played right into their hands. All the promises which Chawki had made on live television in France were crumbling away in the harsh reality of that garden in Yemen. Bernard and Jean-Pierre appeared unsure how to gain control of the situation. They were not going to be able to do any more than record whatever sort of show the Yemenis were preparing to put on for them. They could do nothing to speed things up or influence the situation.

Suddenly Nadia appeared at the entrance to the garden, swathed from head to foot in black. Both Mum and I knew it was her immediately. The cameras started to click and whirr on all sides as she made her way towards us. Her husband, Mohammed, was with her, and he was carrying a child. I clutched Mum's arm.

'Marcus?' I said, hardly daring to believe that they might have brought him to me after all. But even as I spoke his name I knew it wasn't him. It was a little baby, Nadia's latest child.

There was no sign of a boy of six. My heart sank. They were not going to keep their word.

Chawki was talking to Nadia as they approached, whispering into her veiled ear, telling her what to say. Her eyes darted from side to side in the slit of her veil, confused and frightened. The crowd kept their distance, watching silently. The cameras continued snapping and humming, recording the meeting for the media and for the hundreds of official files that must exist on the case. Some of the pictures would surface later in a spread in *Hello!* magazine.

Nadia stopped a few feet in front of us and held her hands out with her palms up. 'What's going on?' she asked us, her voice trembling with fear.

'What do you mean?' Mum asked.

'What's all this?' She gestured at the crowds of men and cameras. 'Why are all this lot here?'

'It's not us, Nard,' Mum said. 'It's them. They promised that we'd be able to visit you, all the children and Marcus. Where are all the kids?'

Nadia flashed an angry look at Mohammed. 'They're all at school,' she spat.

The officials, including Chawki, had gathered at the gate, blocking us from making a run for it. God knows where they thought we would go.

I forced myself to walk across to Mohammed and greet him politely. I admired the child. I tried to think how a long-lost sister should act in this situation when all her instincts are telling her to hug her sister to her and scream and cry.

A Yemeni cameraman came too close and I snapped at him

46

in Arabic to 'get back to his mother's house'. Nadia giggled and for a moment it was like the old days, when I used to protect her and we used to get into mischief together. Then she reverted to being the brain-washed zombie from Mokbana, the woman who had learnt to cut herself off from all the pain and unhappiness.

We sat down in a semi-circle of hard chairs. Nadia uncovered her face and I started talking to her. I just let it all pour out. Mum and I were both shocked by how thin and drained she looked. For half an hour we sat together in the garden as I tried to tell her as much as possible about what was going on. I could see she was confused. It was all too complicated to be explained in such a short space of time, especially in such a tense situation. Mohammed hovered nervously around us, casting anxious glances at the men who watched over us all.

Mum followed my lead and asked me to tell Mohammed that she accepted him as a son-in-law. I passed the message on but he seemed uninterested in anything we had to say – contemptuous even. Jean-Pierre stepped forward to do the interview. With the cameras on her, Nadia covered her face again, her eyes wide with anxiety as she started to spout the lines which they had taught her so carefully.

'I am a Muslim,' she said. 'I am happy here. I would like to visit England with my husband and children, but without the fuss. If the media stop their attentions we can come.'

'The media took no notice for four years,' Mum interrupted, unable to contain herself. 'If the spotlight is turned off now, things will go back to the beginning and nothing will happen.'

'We will never give up trying to get you out,' I insisted, but it was like talking to someone in a trance. I wanted to shake her and bring her to her senses. She went back to speaking her lines like some child reciting in a school play. Jean-Pierre interrupted her with a question which obviously hadn't been in the script which they had made her learn.

'Would you like to go to Birmingham, Nadia?'

She stopped talking and a look of panic came into her eyes. A camera snapped the moment and the image of her eyes in that second would eventually become the cover for new editions of the book all over the world, a terrible, haunting picture of sadness.

'It's not possible,' she said.

'What do you mean?' Jean-Pierre persisted.

'It's not possible, because of all this.' She gestured towards all the people standing around.

'What can you remember of England?' Jean-Pierre asked.

'I was only little,' she faltered. 'I was only small. I was only eleven, twelve, thirteen.'

Mohammed was becoming frantic with nerves, saying that they had to get back to the other children in the village, that we must hurry up and get the whole thing over. He must have been under a lot of pressure from his father and from the authorities. The poor man must have rued the day that his father came back to Yemen with a foreign bride for him. There must have been many times when he wished that he had married a cousin from the village, a girl whose family would be happy about the marriage and would give him no trouble. As it was, his fate had been sealed by his father and he had to make the best of it.

Even if he had wanted to come to England with his family, I doubt if his father would have allowed it. At that moment, however, I felt no sympathy for him. As far as I was concerned, he was Nadia's husband and he was now the one standing between her and freedom.

'Where's Marcus?' I wanted to know.

'His grandfather would not allow him to come,' an official told me, and I remembered the spite and tyranny with which both Abdul Khada and Gowad used to rule their families. I felt sick with sadness for my lost son.

'They said I could see him!' I was so angry I couldn't cry. 'They said that if I wanted him I could fight for him in the courts here.'

The officials shrugged, exchanged glances and hid their amused smiles badly. 'There is no way for you to do that,' they told me.

I felt my rage building. In a way I was angry with myself for letting them get my hopes up, even that small amount. I should have known by now that government officials will say anything that suits them at that moment, whatever country they are from.

Mum and I were asked to wait in a nearby room while the rest of the interview was conducted. A line of chairs was set out and four local women sat down directly opposite us. They were veiled like Nadia and every time Mum or I whispered to each other they craned forward to hear what we were saying. These women stayed with us for the rest of our visit. We couldn't even visit the toilet without them escorting us. The officials were not about to take any chances at all. They wanted us to know that they were in charge.

When the interview was complete, Mohammed grudgingly agreed to let Nadia come in the jeep with Mum and me for the ten-minute ride to the hotel where we were to rest until flying out.

In the privacy of the car, as we drove through the dusty, bustling streets, she opened up a little and asked after friends in England. We showed her some photos we had brought with us. She began to cry softly.

'I would like to come back,' she whispered, 'and they say I can leave with you now, but I cannot take the children. I can't leave them. I can't endanger their lives. The men are threatening me all the time, telling me what I must say. I just want to be left alone.'

We reached the hotel and were given a few minutes to talk, but the time we had been promised alone with Nadia never happened. Everyone stayed with us and when Mohammed stood up and ordered her to follow, she rose and obediently fell into step two paces behind him.

'Nadia,' Mum called after her. 'Please, Nadia!'

'I have to go now, Mum,' she said, and I could see the tears in her eyes as she walked away.

Chawki appeared, with his arms folded, smirking. Mum flew at him in a rage. 'You promised me I would see my grandchildren,' she screamed.

'Why not go to the village?' he suggested casually.

'No.' I froze, horrified at the thought of going back to that place, knowing that we would never get out alive. 'Never!'

'You can,' Chawki was teasing us. 'You and your mother. You have a problem with this, Zana?'

I went mad, hurling every Arabic profanity I could come up with at his head. He ran for it without another word. I could see Nadia outside, getting into a Land Rover. I ran to catch up, unable to bear the thought of her going without saying another word.

'I love you, Nard,' I cried.

Nadia leant forward to kiss me. 'I love you all,' she said in her Brummie accent.

I hugged her to me and she whispered in my ear. 'Zane, did you forget me? Please don't forget me. You promised you never would. Don't leave me here. Not too long, please.' She gripped my arms and breathed deeply to control her tears.

'I'll never forget you, Nard. You'll be home soon. You don't know what's been going on in Europe, but I'm getting you out. It doesn't matter how but you're coming out.'

'I know,' she said. 'I understand.'

She knows me like nobody else does and she knows that I will not give up until I have got her back to England. She knew then that I hadn't forgotten her. She had been talking in anger and confusion. She knew that I would never forget her.

The French team were all deeply shocked and disappointed with the way things had turned out. I think everyone else had thought that even if we weren't able to bring Nadia back on the plane with us, at least we would receive a promise that she would be able to follow us within a few days or weeks. I had wanted to believe the same, but in my heart I knew that it was going to be harder than that.

The moment I was back in Yemen, the moment I saw all those men with their guns, when I had to listen to their double-talk, I knew that they weren't going to give her up. We might be able to talk to her in front of the cameras for a few minutes, but they had her in their power for years. They could make her say or do anything they wanted. They could threaten her with losing her children or with beatings. I knew, in my heart, that it was going to take us much longer than this to get her out.

I couldn't resist reminding the others that this was exactly how I had predicted the whole thing would turn out. Chawki invited us all to a 'banquet' which had been set up in our honour. Mum and I told him to stuff his banquet and went back to our hotel room to weep in private. At that moment it seemed as if there was no hope at all.

3

'Why Can't I Have a Life Like My Sisters?'

It would be impossible to live for long without hope. Even when all my dreams have been dashed by some setback or disappointment, a small seed of hope is always germinating in the back of my mind, putting down roots, watered by my tears and growing slowly to replace whatever has been lost. Each new hope gives me a reason to keep on fighting.

In the excitement of the publicity in Paris, I had allowed my hopes to grow too high. Despite all my suspicions and reservations a part of me had begun to believe that miracles might be possible. I was bound to come down to earth with a painful crash. I had allowed myself to believe that the media coverage was actually going to make a difference. It had been the media, after all, in the shape of the *Observer*, that had got me out of Yemen and had brought our plight to the attention of the authorities and the public.

53

I had felt sure that if we could just get enough journalists on our side we would be bound to succeed. Everyone always talks about 'the power of the media' and the pressure which it can bring to bear on governments and organisations. How could we fail, I thought, when tens of millions of people in Europe were backing us up? How could the British and Yemeni governments fail to respond to such a force?

In Taiz, away from the adrenaline and excitement of television studios, airports and media conferences in five-star hotel suites, our efforts had done little more than annoy and embarrass the Yemenis.

The men who had surrounded us in that sad little walled garden had never heard of the *Observer* or *Sacrée Soirée*. It meant nothing to them that tens of millions of Europeans had read or heard our story and believed that we were being treated wrongly. They only knew what they were told by their own media and government. They had been told that Mum and I had overturned their traditions and made a mockery of them. They saw only a couple of troublesome women trying to make things uncomfortable for them, questioning the way they had always led their lives and challenging their right to do as they pleased with the women in their families. Although we had successfully shown them that we were not entirely powerless and that we were determined to fight on, there was still a long struggle ahead.

Back in the *Sacrée Soirée* studio in Paris, Chawki was triumphant. Nadia had repeated all the phrases to the cameras that they wanted. 'You can see for yourself . . .' he crowed. 'Just listen to her.' But the audience had seen the hurt in Nadia's eyes on the screens and they hissed him again.

The people watching could tell that Nadia was talking under duress. If a woman is beaten by her husband, it is likely that she will deny it but her eyes will speak the truth. No one looking at Nadia's eyes that day could believe that she was telling the truth when she said that she was happy and wanted to be left alone with her 'good' husband. And at no stage in the proceedings had she ever said she didn't want to return to England, she merely said that it was 'impossible', because of 'them'. The French public was not fooled. They understood what Nadia was telling them.

But Chawki, like a slippery lawyer in court, had an answer for every argument that Jean-Pierre put to him. He denied that they had promised to bring the children to Taiz for the meeting. He claimed that they were waiting for us in the village and that I had refused to go and see them. He denied that there was anything odd about children so young having to go to school.

When Jean-Pierre asked if he didn't think it was more important for the children to see their grandmother and aunt after four years, Chawki claimed that we had been shouting at one another and that Nadia had been blaming Mum for all the trouble. He saw this as evidence that we were not a close family at all, rather that it was Nadia and Mohammed who were close. We were troublemakers, trying to come between a husband and wife.

The argument just went round and round in circles. Chawki was like a snake and the audience were becoming angrier and more aggressive towards him with each twist of his tongue and each slippery evasion and half-truth.

He kept saying that Nadia was a grown-up and had to be allowed to make her own choices — as if we were the ones forcing her to do something she didn't want to do, as if we were trying to drag her back to England against her will.

The French press weren't fooled either and the next day they were full of sadness at what they had seen through the camera. In their eyes Nadia was still a little girl who was being held against her will as her life ebbed away from her in an endless grind of toil and repression. They had all seen the dark, tragic eyes peering out of the veil as if it were a cage which had become a haven for its timid inmate from the frightening outside world.

A few months later Ashia, my younger sister, bumped into Dad in a street in Birmingham. I imagine he is always pleased to be able to talk to one of the others in the family because it allows him to let us know things when we won't talk to him ourselves.

He told Ashia that Nadia was happy, was pregnant again and had been given £10,000 by the Yemeni government as some sort of compensation. This is an incredible amount of money in Yemen. If this is true, it shows that their consciences troubled them.

Even if such a payment had been made, of course, none of the money would have reached Nadia. What would she have been able to do with money in Ashube? There were no banks for her to pay it into. She had no way of controlling or spending money. The men would have taken it on her behalf and that would have been the last she saw of it. It would have disappeared into late-night card games. It would have bought quat, the drug they all chew day in and day out, or it might have bought some other man's daughters.

When Bernard Fixot rang Mum to find out how we were, she told him what Ashia had discovered. He was amazed by the news and arranged for Ashia and me to be invited back on to *Sacrée Soirée*. I happily accepted the invitation. It was like going back to visit old friends. The thought of appearing on live television no longer worried me.

Jean-Pierre wanted to find out what had happened since the last show. He couldn't believe that we had not moved a single step closer to our goal.

This time Chawki was not invited to appear, but as soon as the live broadcast started, he rang the station in a rage. He must have been watching it at his home and dashed straight over to defend himself and his beloved country. I guess he had expected that we would give up and settle down after the disappointments of the visit to Taiz. He must have been horrified to find that we were still fighting. I dare say he had boasted to his bosses that he had sorted out the whole affair, and now we were going to show him up as a liar on national television.

Halfway through the show he arrived at the studio, puffing and panting from exertion, to refute what we were saying. All the same arguments started up again. He was brimming with indignation, saying that we should be grateful to the Yemeni government for getting Nadia and me out of the villages as soon as they were aware of our plight, and for getting me to England when I asked to leave.

He said he had been responsible for the meeting in the garden in Taiz, and that we were showing him no gratitude.

They were all the same weasel words we had heard before, but this time he had had less time to prepare what he was going to say and it was even more obvious to the audience that he was in the wrong.

He hadn't changed his position. He said we should stop selling the book because we were poisoning people's minds, and the Yemeni government had more important things to do than worry about us. He gave the impression that we were troublemakers and that we were just trying to make money from Nadia's misfortune. The audience was as antagonistic as ever but this time I knew that it would make no difference. This time I didn't allow my hopes to be raised too high. I was now prepared for a long haul and I was going to pace myself better.

If one good thing had come out of our struggles and the publicity which they generated, it was that Dad and his friends had not been able to get to Ashia, Tina or Mo — despite threats which they had made in the early days to kidnap them and take them to Yemen.

Both Ashia and Tina were settling down to lives in Birmingham. Tina had two kids by then and Ashia was expecting her second. Their lives were just as they wanted them to be, free and peaceful. They were with good men who treated them well and respected them. If Nadia had been there it would have been the happiest of times for our family as Mum became a grandmother over and over again.

I was living comfortably in my flat and I was able to give Liam everything that I had never had when I was a child. I didn't need any more than that. We were a happy little family unit, Liam and me.

Liam's dad, Jimmy, and I had drifted apart. We were still good friends and Liam and I saw a lot of him and his family, but Jimmy had found living with me too much of a strain. I know I was very moody and difficult. When I arrived back from Yemen, I was so messed up psychologically that there was little chance I would be able to sustain a relationship with anyone. Both of us had changed in the eight years we had been apart.

I was so wrapped up in my own grief and emotional turmoil that I didn't have any reserves left to share with a partner. I wasn't able to think about what he must have been through in that time. We both needed looking after at the same time but neither of us was in a strong enough state to be of help to the other.

Jimmy had always been a great friend of mine and all the years that I was in Yemen with Nadia he had kept a picture of me in his wallet. But each day that we were together in England we could feel that we were slowly falling apart. We wanted to stay friends, and I wanted him around for Liam, and so we parted on good terms.

When Liam was two, Jimmy suggested that we should all go down to St Kitts the following year with his family for a long holiday. It would mean that Liam would get to meet more of his relations and we would have a wonderful holiday at the same time. I thought it sounded like a great idea and we went ahead and booked the tickets. I started to look forward to a holiday in the Caribbean with my son and his family.

By that time I was seeing a lot of Paul, who was part of the same circle of friends. His family was from St Kitts as well.

Nine months before we were all due to go on our trip I fell pregnant with Cyan. When I found out, and realised that the dates were going to overlap, I knew that I wasn't going to be able to go.

I had been having a lot of trouble with pregnancies. Both before and after Liam I had miscarriages. There were nine of them in all. The doctors told me it was because the lining of my womb was weak, but I believe it stems from the time they gave me a D and C in Yemen (which they did without an anaesthetic). Sometimes I wonder why I went on tormenting my body by trying to get pregnant during those times. I have no explanation other than that I was meant to have the kids I now have.

Two years after Cyan was born I went to the doctor for a sterilisation. It seemed a sensible move, after all I now had one child in Yemen and two in Birmingham. But something inside my head was telling me that it was the wrong thing to do. I felt torn in half.

I told the doctor that I had changed my mind, that I couldn't explain why but it didn't feel right any more. He was furious. He told me that I had wasted his time and taken up an appointment which someone else could have had. I just walked away. I knew it felt like the right thing to do. Soon afterwards I discovered I was pregnant again, with Mark. I was already pregnant that day in the doctor's surgery, although I didn't know it. I guess that was why my body was telling me not to go ahead with the operation. Thank God I didn't because Mark is a joy — despite being the naughtiest child I have had so far!

When I discovered I was pregnant with Cyan, I had already

lost two sets of twins and I was told that I was now expecting a third set. Yet again I started to miscarry, but this time I only lost one of the babies. The other I continued to carry to full term.

Cyan, my little miracle baby, was due in November and that was when the holiday was booked, but I still wanted Liam to have the experience, even if I couldn't be there. It would be great for him to spend some time with his dad, and to see his country.

Deep in the recesses of my mind warning bells sounded. What if Jimmy decided to keep Liam down there? What if this was history repeating itself? Was I being a fool to agree to such a thing?

I decided to quell the voices. I had known Jimmy and his family for twenty years and I trusted them all completely. I was almost as close to them as I was to my own family. This was not like my father and his cronies. And anyway, this was the West Indies, not the Middle East.

By the time Liam and Jimmy left for the Caribbean I was almost ready to go into labour, which took my mind off any other worries I might have had. A few days later I gave birth to Cyan.

Nothing about the birth was a problem. As with Liam, I had refused to take anything for pain control because I didn't see why I should have it when Nadia didn't. I've also come to believe that natural births are the best way to do things if it's possible and if there are skilled medical people and equipment available should any complications develop.

Liam was going to be in St Kitts for six weeks, which gave

me the perfect opportunity (more or less forty days, as the tradition goes in Yemen) to spend some quiet time with my new baby. It was a lovely time for me. I spoke to Liam almost every day on the phone, and ended up with a £400 phone bill as a result. I could tell from his voice just what a great time he was having.

It was worth paying the phone bill to be able to keep my worries about Liam at bay so that I could enjoy Cyan to the full and be refreshed and ready for Liam when he exploded back into my life, sporting a really dark tan. By that time Cyan was smiling and I was back on my feet with no pain left.

I knew how lucky I was to be able to have my baby in a free society, compared with the conditions in which Marcus, and all Nadia's children, had been born. At some moments it made me indescribably happy to enjoy the luxuries of living in my little two-bedroom flat with my children, enough money to give them whatever they needed and all my friends and my family around me.

Then, just as I might be relaxing a bit, I would be struck by a shaft of guilt about Nadia, and about Marcus who had lost his mum when he was so little. How could I be allowed to be so happy with Liam and Cyan, when Marcus must have gone through so much sadness after I left him?

By now he was almost a man in Yemeni eyes and I knew I wouldn't have recognised him if he had walked into the room. I had not seen any pictures of him since I left. All I had to remember was a miserable, waif-like, two-year-old infant.

My moods continued to swing back and forth as they always did, but I made sure that I didn't cry in front of the kids. I didn't want them growing up thinking their mum was always miserable during their childhoods. I had a good example of this in Mum. Although I now know how hard Dad made her life when we were young, she never let us feel that there was anything wrong. She always put on a brave face, and as a result she has brought up a bunch of very self-confident people. The fact that our family is so unhappy at its core is because of outside forces, never because of the way Mum behaved. I would like my children to be able to say the same about me one day.

As it was, Mum was too distracted, worried and angry to enjoy her grandchildren as she should have. It was impossible for her to settle down to anything as long as she knew that one of her own children was lost to her and needed help. We could all see the toll it was taking on her health, which had never been good. She began to suffer from agoraphobia and rarely left the house, not that that stopped her from her determined struggle to get Nadia back.

She was constantly trying to find new avenues, telephoning and making new contacts, going over and over everything that had happened since 1980 with anyone who would listen, searching for some explanation for why it had all gone so wrong, praying that some break would appear in the clouds.

In her searches she had met a woman called Jana Wain through an organisation for mothers who have lost their children, called Reunite.

Mum and Jana forged an incredibly close bond. Mum started to go out and about with Jana, something which we had begun to think we would never see her do again. Jana called it 'networking', and it did Mum a great deal of good to hear that there were so many other people in a similar position to herself. Mum felt safe with Jana. She knew that whatever happened Jana would be there for her, that she was as dedicated to saving Nadia as Mum and I were.

A few months after the trip to Taiz with the French camera crew, Mum shocked us with an announcement that she was planning to go down to Yemen again to visit Nadia properly. This time she didn't want to be accompanied by the media. She didn't want to make any fuss. She just wanted to present herself as a mother visiting her daughter and grandchildren.

She had been horrified to hear that Nadia was pregnant again and wanted to be there to help her when the baby arrived. She knew she couldn't go alone and she wanted to find a man who would accompany her. A man would get more respect, both from the Yemenis themselves and from the people at the British embassy. He would also be able to provide Mum with some physical protection should she need it.

She approached several male friends and some of them said they would be happy to go with her, but they all had jobs and had to give notice if they wanted time off. Mum didn't think she could wait. She was frantic with worry about Nadia and couldn't be sure how long it would be before the baby was due. In a despairing phone call to Jana, she poured out all her problems and Jana offered to accompany her. Although Mum was loath to take advantage of such a good friend she could see no alternative and took her up on the offer.

When I heard what they were planning to do, I was very nervous for them and, as it turned out, my fears proved well founded. Mum told me she wanted to be able to talk to Nadia without all the pressure of the media, to spend some time with her, trying to find out what Nadia truly wanted and looking for a way to make it happen. Most of all, Mum wanted to help Nadia with the children while she was giving birth.

'Jana has said she will travel with me,' Mum told me. 'We've been to the embassy, and got our visas and everything. You won't believe what they said to Jana when she first rang them. She spoke to a senior Foreign Office person. He told her that it was the Foreign Office's opinion that we should leave Nadia in peace, that it was unfair to disturb her and the children just to appease the mother. He said, "This is a matter between husband and wife. We have always made our view clear, that this is a family matter."'

Jana was shocked to learn that the British officials took much the same view of the situation as Chawki and his fellow Yemenis, even though we had been telling her that that was the sort of attitude we had been fighting from the beginning. If anything, however, it made Jana more determined to help Mum. Certainly neither of them were going to allow it to put them off. (If Mum had given up every time someone told her it was a waste of time I would still be living in Yemen and neither Nadia nor I would have heard from her after 1980.)

The Foreign Office had first taken the attitude that they should not interfere when we were still two British children — one of whom should legally have been attending school in Britain. As the years rolled by, and the case became more complicated, their opinions had hardened against us. We were, it seemed, too much of an inconvenience.

Once they had their visas, Mum prepared a suitcase of things for Nadia and we all helped her to fill it. We packed Nadia's favourite cheese and onion crisps, packets of Toffos, tins of tomato soup, all the things which we knew she had loved when she lived in England and wouldn't have had for years. We put in books in English to keep her memory of the language alive, even though we knew she rarely had a chance to speak it any more. We put together a collection of mementoes and photographs of friends and family to convince her that she was not forgotten and that we would never abandon her – though the months might tick away and it might seem that nothing was happening. We bought toys for her kids and for Marcus.

Before Mum left, I sat down with a tape recorder and made a tape. I explained in detail everything that was happening. It is hard to talk into a tape recorder when the person you are speaking to isn't there and you have no way of knowing their reactions to the things you are saying. I tried to anticipate every question she would ask if I could talk to her face to face, but I'm sure I must have left a lot of gaps and rambled on about things she had no interest in.

As the day of their departure drew near, I became more and more frightened for Mum. I knew that she was going to be in physical danger the moment she stepped out of the airport, but I had great faith in Jana. She was a strong and intelligent woman. She was very good at keeping Mum calm and often prevented her from acting without thinking. If she was safe with any woman, that person was Jana. As it was, not even Jana could protect Mum from what was to come.

*

Mum knew just what she was letting herself in for – she had been to Yemen several times by then in her efforts to get us out. But Jana still had no idea what to expect. She seemed to think they would just be able to visit Nadia for some nice get-togethers. She didn't understand that there would always be armed men around, or that they would be lied to at every turn by everyone they came in contact with. She didn't appreciate that promises would be made to them every day that would vanish into thin air a few hours later; that appointments would be postponed and postponed and postponed; that men would smile and smile as they were plotting to outwit and humiliate them.

Despite the fact that Jana had heard the opinion of a Foreign Office official in Britain, she still thought that once she and Mum were there, they would receive help from the British embassy. I tried to warn her as best I could, believing that corruption showed in all walks of life. I tried to prepare her for the days and weeks she was likely to spend waiting by the phone for promised calls that would never come, and the guarantees that everyone would make and then shrug off a few days later. I tried to explain that as a Western woman she would not be able to walk the streets of Taiz freely, that she would feel threatened and despised wherever she went, and that she would end up staying in the hotel room rather than face one more humiliating leer or shouted insult in a public place.

I suspect she grew quite tired of my pessimism and hoped that she would be able to prove me wrong. I hoped she would too. Our whole family was deeply grateful to Jana for the support that she was showing for Mum. No one else had given up so much of their time so selflessly for us.

Finally, their day of departure came. I gave Mum a big hug as we said goodbye, fearful that this might be the last time I saw her. My mood wavered between telling myself not to be so melodramatic and the stomach-sinking realisation that people disappeared all the time in Yemen and no one was ever the wiser.

Once they had gone, I tried to keep in regular contact with them by phone from the flat. It was a constant struggle and my phone bill went through the roof. The phone lines were bad anyway, but Mum and Jana also had to change hotels because they were being followed and threatened. Wherever they were, messages never seemed to get through to them.

Every time I had trouble contacting them panic gripped my insides. I was certain that they had been killed or spirited away into the mountains. Whenever I did get through, Mum would be uncommunicative. She was certain that the phone lines were bugged. I'm sure she was right. I could often hear men's voices talking in Arabic in the background and there were always a lot of clicks on the line. I wanted to be told what was going on, but I knew better than to interrogate Mum on the phone. It was enough just to know that they were alive for another day.

I did not find out the whole truth of what had happened to them until much later. From the moment they landed in Sana'a things went badly. Everyone seemed to know a suspicious amount about our story, almost as if they had been briefed to keep an eye on Jana and Mum.

I could imagine the impact which Jana was having on the men. She is very tall, with bright auburn hair. She would stick out wherever they went amongst the dark, shrouded local women. She was drawing exactly the sort of unwelcome attention from the men that I had warned her about. After a few days, Mum confessed to me that they had decided to cover themselves in veils and long dresses in order to melt into the background. It made me laugh to think of them dressing themselves up. I knew that Jana would still be towering above most other women, so no one would have any trouble spotting her.

When I rang a few days later I could tell that something had gone horribly wrong. Mum was talking strangely, as if badly frightened. I insisted that she give me an idea of what had happened.

'I told Jimmy (a taxi driver who had stuck to them like glue) that I wanted to get to Ashube,' she explained. 'He said he would need a map and he stopped at this shop. He went in for a bit, leaving us in the car. Then he came out and called us to go in as well. They said they couldn't find Ashube on the map. There was this crowd of armed men in the shop, Zane. Then Jimmy shouted out my name and more of them appeared outside.'

My heart was thumping in my chest as I listened to this story. Eventually there were about fifty men there and they began to get very aggressive. They all knew the story of 'the sad sisters of Mokbana' and they seemed to believe that Mum had come to take Nadia back. They told her what a bad woman she was and seemed ready to attack her. They jostled forward, hemming her in, pushing and shoving and making threats.

Mum and Jana realised that they were in serious danger and they pushed their way through the crowd, fleeing from the shop back to Jimmy's car which was parked outside. Jimmy went with them, climbing quickly into the driving seat. Maybe he too was surprised by the ferocity of the crowd's mood and didn't want Mum or Jana to actually be harmed whilst in his care.

The scent of fear brought out the mob's primitive hunting instincts. They became increasingly angry. They shouted and jeered abuse and circled round the car to stop it from moving.

Once Mum and Jana had locked themselves into the back seats the crowd began to rock the Mercedes back and forth, making angry death threats through the windows, scraping knives across their throats to show what would happen to Mum if she persisted in trying to see Nadia, sneering and snarling, their ugly mouths full of quat-stained teeth.

Jimmy was panicking badly now. The attackers were climbing all over the roof, boot and bonnet of the car. As he started the engine and tried to move forward, one of them tore open the unlocked passenger door and climbed in. Jimmy fought with him as the car began to gather speed, holding on to the steering wheel with his free hand. He eventually managed to force the man back out of the door into the road and sped away before anyone else could catch them up.

I was hearing my worst nightmares recounted to me.

'They want you to know that you're not welcome in Yemen,' I told Mum.

'I already know that, Zane.' I could tell she was crying. 'Do you think I don't already know that?'

'You can't go to Mokbana, Mum,' I pleaded. 'They'll kill you if you try. Once you are out of the town they can do whatever they want with you. There must be thousands of men who would be happy to do the job.'

I begged her to come home, but there was no chance of persuading her. She had gone to see Nadia and she would not change her plans just because people wanted her to, however frightened she might feel.

We all knew that Nadia was getting closer and closer to her due date and I could understand why Mum was determined to be there to support her. I felt the same desperate urge to rush over to protect my baby sister from danger, but I knew there was nothing I could do. As long as there was a possibility that Mum could do something to help, I had to give her my support. I knew that, with or without it, she was not going to change her mind at this stage.

We both knew, from my experiences, just how primitive, dangerous and painful childbirth was in the villages. We also knew that Nadia had been advised by doctors not to have any more children. The thought of just how dangerous the forthcoming birth was going to be was chilling.

The trouble had started when Nadia gave birth to Tina. She was an enormous baby, with a full head of long dark hair. The village women had tried to help Nadia to get her out the natural way, but it eventually became obvious that Tina was stuck. There was a razor blade which the women kept for circumcising both the baby boys and girls. They never sterilised it. They simply put it away in a jar between uses. When they realised that there was a chance they might lose both Tina and

71

Nadia if they did not act decisively, they got out the unster-
ilised blade and made a long ragged cut which allowed Tina to
be born. They had no way of disinfecting the wound and so
it had never healed properly. Nadia's husband, however, had
continued to take his conjugal rights and had continued to
make her pregnant. Her daily workload became heavier as
her family increased.

The thought of poor Nadia being put through such an
ordeal again, and possibly even losing her life, without anyone
she loved being there to help, was unbearable for me and Mum.
At least Mum was in Yemen. She was doing something. I felt
completely helpless. I was terrified that I would never see
either of them again. I started to develop alopecia. My hair
began coming out in bundles if I so much as touched it. I was
thinking about the two of them every minute of every day. If
I managed to nod off during the night I would have terrible
dreams, never quite sure when I was awake or asleep.

I knew that no man could have deterred Mum from trying
to get to her daughter. Anyone who has seen a lioness protecting her young will know that a mother in this position is an
awesome force. I had to think about Liam and how to protect
him now. That meant I couldn't go to Yemen and risk my life
even if I managed to pluck up the courage. I couldn't see a way
forward.

The staff at the British embassy and the Governor of Taiz
added their warnings to the ones Mum had heard from me,
but I expect by that stage they knew her well enough to know
she was not likely to take any notice of anything they might
say.

Behind the scenes, the British diplomats must have been talking to the Yemenis about the situation, telling them that Mum was determined to see Nadia and was unlikely to go away until she was satisfied. The Yemenis must have realised that she was not going to take no for an answer and that if they organised a meeting to placate her, they stood a better chance of getting her on a plane back to England. They told Mum that they would bring Nadia to Taiz, with Mohammed and the children, for a family reunion.

When Nadia arrived, she had Tina and Haney with her, but not the two smaller children. I was ringing Mum every few hours to try to find out what was happening. I hated being so far away from them when they were together. Eventually I got through to Mum and I could tell that things had not gone well. Her voice was sad and listless. She sounded exhausted. She told me the atmosphere was poisoned from the start. Nadia, who was obviously tired, ill and under pressure from everyone around her, was suspicious of Jana, thinking she was another journalist, there to cause more trouble.

From Nadia's point of view, every time Mum or I organised some publicity outside Yemen, she was given a hard time by the men in her life. Although she knew that we were doing it all for her benefit, she must have dreaded the consequences each time we were successful in raising media interest in her story. The more pressure we put on the Yemenis, the more pressure they put on her. She had never met Jana and she immediately assumed the worst.

'When Nard got here,' Mum told me, 'Faisal barged in with

her.' Faisal Abdul Aziz was the Governor of Taiz's oily assistant. He had obviously been given the job of clearing up the whole business as quickly as possible.

'He had a bunch of armed men with him,' she went on. 'They were such greedy pigs. They ate all the sweets that I had laid out on the bed for the kids.'

I could picture the scene exactly. I had had to deal with men like that all the time when I had been out there. Faisal would have exhibited the same bullying behaviour as Chawki had in Paris. However, he had none of the restraining factors imposed on Chawki, who was watched by television cameras and the press. Faisal would have felt free to bully, hector, smirk and swagger all he liked. He was, after all, only dealing with women – and foreign women at that. I felt furious and impotent at the same time. I couldn't even get to the man to tell him exactly what I thought of him.

'We couldn't talk about anything personal with so many people in the room,' Mum explained. 'So Jana told the men that she wanted to change her clothes so would they please leave the room.'

I laughed. I knew that Arab men would find it difficult to know how to deal with a flame-haired woman who was taller than many of them and showed no fear.

'Did they go?' I asked.

'Yes.'

'Then what happened?'

'Nard took her veil off and we relaxed for a few minutes. I was able to get a much better look at her than when we came over with the French. She looks so old, Zane.' I could hear

Mum's voice cracking as she talked about her child. 'Her skin is so weather-beaten and pock-marked. It's like old leather.'

If every day you are working in the burning sun or bending over the intense heat of a primitive stove, you are bound to change. If your diet is dry and monotonous and you never get enough sleep, your skin is going to age at twice the rate of someone who does not have to endure such hardship.

It was Nadia's eyes, however, that told the full story of how hard her life had been. The pictures which the photographers in the walled garden had taken had been flashed all around the world when we got back, and it was the image of Nadia's sad eyes staring out from inside the veil which had made the most dramatic impact on everyone who saw them. In many countries, including Britain, the publishers of *Sold* had scrapped their existing front covers and used that haunting image instead.

Mum showed Nadia the pictures of all of us that we had packed for her. Jana told me later that there were tears in Nadia's eyes as she pored over each snap, staring at the happy, laughing faces as people hammed it up for the cameras.

'Why can't I have a life like my sisters?' she asked. Neither Jana nor Mum had any answer for her.

The faces of her brother and sisters must have looked strange to her, adults that she was seeing for the first time who bore a ghost-like resemblance to the children she had left behind in 1980. Apart from seeing Mo when he came out with Mum the first time, after we had been away for six years, she had not seen them since she set off on what she thought was to be a few weeks holiday in Yemen.

75

It is now nearly twenty years since my three younger sisters have seen each other. All of them are struggling to hold on to memories of one another which must be fading and changing with time. Nadia must find it hard to imagine what Ashia and Tina's lives are like in England, just as I know they have trouble imagining what Nadia's endless days of monotonous toil in Yemen must be like.

Mum and I have never tried to exclude Ashia or Tina from anything that was going on, but at the same time we have tried to spare them as much of the suffering as possible. Why should we make them as unhappy as we have been if there is no benefit to be had from it? They have suffered because we have suffered, but at the same time they have been able to lead normal Western lives, having children with the men of their choice and living where they want.

We all live near to one another in Birmingham and we see each other all the time. Our children are close with all their English cousins, but none of them can imagine how their Yemeni cousins in Ashube live. It is like two different worlds, linked only by the few photographs which travel back and forth between us on our pain-filled journeys.

'Why don't you come to the embassy with us now?' Mum asked Nadia that day when they were sitting together in the hotel room. 'We'll arrange for your passport and you can fly home to England with us.'

'It's not me, Mum,' Nadia said. 'It's them.' She gestured towards the door and the men waiting outside to take her away again.

At the end of half an hour, when it still felt to them as if they were only just starting to talk properly, Mohammed poked his head through the door and said in Arabic, 'Come on, bitch!' Nadia silently gathered up the children and left the room with him.

When Mum told me that one word, I knew what Mohammed and Nadia's relationship must be like. I could imagine how she must look forward to him going off on trips or taking jobs overseas, and how she must dread his return home. I could picture how he would abuse and belittle her in front of the children, and how she would have learnt to shut out all feelings rather than allow his insults to reach her soul.

Even though Nadia had been swept away from them prematurely, Mum and Jana felt a little more optimistic now that they knew Nadia was in the city. Although they had only been allowed half an hour with her that day, maybe they would be able to spend more time with her later, when the men were less nervous and protective. Once they were sure that Jana was just a friend and not a journalist, when they had accepted the idea that Nadia simply wanted to spend some time with her mother, perhaps they would start to allow them to pass several hours at a time together. Mohammed might even see it as a way to keep her and the children busy while he enjoyed a social life in the city. Over the coming weeks they might be able to build enough of a bond of trust with Nadia that she would become less afraid and more willing to think about escaping.

It occurred to them that they might also be able to keep her in Taiz until the birth of the baby, which would mean that they would be able to use the facilities of the hospital. If that happened, trained doctors and midwives would be able to have a look at the damage she had sustained during Tina's birth and help her to ease the pain. Even though they were angry that the meeting had been brutally short and that Faisal and Mohammed had constantly interrupted them, they felt they had taken a step forward. Mum didn't tell me exactly what her plans were over the phone. She knew that they were listening to our conversation. But I guessed from the things she did say, and I prayed that it would work out as she wanted.

Our hopes were soon dashed. The next day, after they had waited in vain for Nadia to be brought back to the hotel, they were told that she had been taken back to the village.

Every time I rang I heard about more meetings that had been arranged and then postponed, more promises that had been made and then broken. I began to despair. Hearing it down long-distance phone lines made it all the more obvious that nothing had changed. I began to feel that the whole trip was going to prove futile. Mum and Jana clutched at every straw they were offered, despite the fact that their hopes were continually being raised and dashed. And all the time we were horribly aware that the days were grinding relentlessly towards the birth of Nadia's next child.

Eventually Mum was told that Nadia couldn't leave the village and come to Taiz because of ill health. Mum made it clear that she was not going back to England until she saw her daughter again. If that meant waiting until after the birth then so be it.

Her complaint against Faisal had been taken seriously by the Governor, who told Faisal off in front of Mum and Jana for the insensitive way in which he had conducted the meeting with Nadia.

'He was really squirming,' Mum told me.

I could tell that she had got some satisfaction from seeing Faisal torn off a strip, but I also knew that she had made an enemy for life. To be humiliated so by a woman must have cut Faisal's pride to the quick.

Faisal's reprimand seemed to make things even worse. Mum and Jana spent their time trying to contact anyone who might have any influence on the situation. Everyone had a different story to tell and it became impossible to tell what was true and what was lies. All Mum could cling to was a stubborn refusal to go without seeing Nadia again.

Some weeks later, as Mum and Jana were coming back to the hotel after dinner one night, Faisal jumped out of a darkened alleyway where he must have been lying in wait. He seemed unusually friendly and told them that there would be a car coming for Mum at five in the morning, which would take her to see Nadia in the village. He said that Nadia was now too heavily pregnant to travel to the city again but that it had been arranged for Mum to go to her.

Luckily, Mum managed to ring me that night and told me what had happened. I felt my heart racing at the thought of what might happen if she accepted the invitation.

'You're not going,' I said. 'What's the Governor's assistant doing hanging around in alleyways at night? He's up to something. If you accept that lift, we'll never see you again.'

I knew that it didn't sound right. If she had been going with someone from the British embassy it would have been different. If she went with Faisal and didn't come back, all he would have to do would be to deny all knowledge of the trip. Who would be able to prove otherwise? When I put down the phone that night, I had a cold feeling that they wanted to get rid of her.

4

Two Paces Behind

In recent months the British media have been full of horror stories about kidnaps and murders of foreigners in Yemen. Some tourists have simply disappeared, others were killed when government troops and the kidnappers opened fire on one another. The media have been shocked, but this sort of banditry is nothing new in Yemen. There are always armed tribesmen in the countryside who will rob and murder people. People have always vanished in the mountains, never to be heard of again, but suddenly it has become big news. I have always known that if I went back to the Mokbana region I could very easily be killed. Luckily, Mum and Jana seemed to have grasped that I was not exaggerating when I said they were in great danger.

We were all horrified to hear that Nadia was going to have to have the baby in the village. Mum had tried begging everyone she met to allow Nadia to be brought in to the hospital in Taiz. But all roads led back to Faisal in the Governor's office.

He just laughed at her concerns, dismissing them as the typical hysterics of a mother. In his most patronising manner, he told her not to worry, that the women of the village knew what they were doing, and that Nadia was experienced at giving birth.

It was precisely because of Nadia's previous experiences that we were so worried. We kept telling anyone who would listen that Nadia had been advised by doctors not to have any more children. They shrugged and said that it was too late to worry about that now, as if it was all Nadia's fault for being so careless as to allow herself to fall pregnant again against the advice of doctors. As if she was given any choice in the matter. As if she was allowed to say 'no' to her husband's attentions. As if she could just go to the shop to buy some contraceptives or to the local doctor for a morning-after tablet.

Given that Nadia had no free choice in any of these matters, it seemed only fair that if she had to go through the birth process again she should be allowed to do it in the city. In Taiz there was some hope of getting medical attention if anything went wrong, whereas in the village Nadia had to rely on the skills of the other women.

There is no doubt the village women are experienced in childbirth. Necessity forces them to attend one another's births all through their lives, but that doesn't mean that they know what to do if any complications arise. None of them have medical supplies, not even the most basic antiseptic or sterilising products.

We knew that as long as there were no complications the women would do the best they could. But what if there were complications? What hope would they have of saving Nadia?

We knew that if Nadia died in childbirth the men would merely shrug and put it down to bad luck but Mum would have lost a daughter, I would have lost a sister and her children would be left without a mother. The authorities, however, would have one less administrative headache. They would be rid of us. It appeared, as I mulled over these thoughts back home in England, that all the cards were stacked against Nadia. In fact, it began to seem to me that it was something of a miracle she had survived as many births as she had.

In the darkest hours of the morning, as I sleeplessly tossed and turned, I remembered how terrifying it had been to give birth to Marcus in the village. There was no one to help but Ward, Abdul Khada's ill-tempered wife, and her methods were rough and unkind.

She had refused to believe me at first when I announced that the baby was coming in the middle of the night. Eventually, when I pulled off my trousers and started getting on with it, she grudgingly started rummaging about between my legs with a torch as I screamed in pain and fear.

Then there had been the terrible moment when she had fallen silent and I had no idea what she was doing. The cord had knotted around Marcus's neck. She had had to release it by torchlight with Abdul Khada shouting at her from the background demanding to know what was going wrong with his grandchild. The thought of Nadia having to go through a similar ordeal again, with all the added complications of her poor health, was horrible. I imagined her dying under the strain and the women shrugging at one another, all of them more than aware of the dangers that every woman faces at those moments, but unable to do anything else to save her.

Being so far away from Nadia means that my imagination paints the darkest possible pictures and I have no way of putting my mind at rest. I am sure the limp she has now stems from that terrible razor cut and I can only speculate about what it actually means. The more I speculate the worse it becomes.

Knowing that there is something physically wrong with her which needs treatment is another reason why those who love Nadia the most are desperate to see her get out of Yemen and back to England. She needs to be examined properly, given medical care and the option of proper birth control. Maybe there is nothing that the doctors can do for her, but she deserves to be given the chance. Maybe her worn appearance is simply the product of too much toiling in the sun and the hard life which has worn her down and made her look prematurely old. If we could just have that confirmed it would put all our minds at rest.

If she came to England for a holiday we would all spoil her like mad, even if it was only for a few weeks. We would wait on her hand and foot, feed her all her favourite foods and build her strength back up. She has not had a break in close to twenty years. There are no days off from the jobs of being a wife and mother, no supportive partner to shoulder part of the burden, no parents or parents-in-law to help with the chores or the responsibilities.

Gowad and his wife came to England many years ago,

leaving Nadia to bring up their younger children as well as her own. They told her that her mother-in-law was only going for a holiday and would be back soon, but she never returned. (Why would any woman want to return to that sort of life if she has the option to live in England, in a society where women are free, medical help is available and where there are any number of modern conveniences to help with the preparation of food and the washing of clothes?)

Mum took my advice that night, knowing that I was right. She didn't go down to meet Faisal and the car at five in the morning. It must have been a hard decision for her. I can imagine how she felt because I had a similar choice on the trip with the French film crew. Part of me wanted to go to the village regardless of the dangers. It seemed like the only way I would see Marcus. The other part of me knew that it would be a foolish risk to take and that there would be no guarantees. Once I was there they might let me see him for no more than five minutes – if that.

Being a mother can tear you apart sometimes. On the one hand you are willing to do anything for your children – even die. On the other, you know that if you are dead your last chance of protecting them is gone. I hate to think how Mum must have felt the night she was trapped in Taiz just a few hours' drive away from Nadia. Mum knew Nadia would be going through the trauma of childbirth any day. She also knew that if she tried to get to her she would almost certainly be killed. She must have been able to visualise the car waiting downstairs and been tempted more than once to go down to it.

It is possible, of course, that had she gone down she would have found no sign of Faisal or the car. We shall never know because Mum stayed safely in her hotel room with Jana.

Once she had refused Faisal's offer of a lift to Ashube, it became even harder to make contact with anyone in authority. No doubt Faisal was able to go back to the Governor and report that he had done his best to satisfy Mum, but that she had refused his 'help' at the last minute. Mum's reputation for being a difficult, stubborn woman would have been confirmed yet again. The authorities could put the file at the bottom of the pile once more in the hope that this time we would shut up. It was a vain hope.

'I've heard from the village,' Mum told me a few weeks later.

'Heard what?' My heart missed a beat as I imagined what terrible news might be coming down the phone line now.

'Nard's had her baby. It's a boy.'

'Is she all right?'

'So they say. But they are hardly going to tell me if she isn't, are they?'

At least we knew that Nadia and the baby had survived the birth. We were sure they would have said if either of them had died. Although this was a relief, I still couldn't imagine how Nadia would find the strength to look after a new-born baby on top of all her other duties. If she was alive, there was hope that Mum and Jana would be able to see her again. I was also relieved that it was a boy. It meant that Mum's newest grand-child had a better chance of a happy life in that world where the men have all the rights and the women have none.

When Mum asked for a meeting to be set up, she was told

that Nadia couldn't travel for forty days after the birth, as that was the tradition in Muslim countries.

In fact the tradition is that the new mother goes back to her mother for forty days, before returning to her husband with the baby. The idea is to give the woman a rest and to allow the grandmother to help with the baby in the early days, until the new mother has regained her strength and is ready to perform her marital duties once more.

But this was contrary to what they were telling Mum. If they really wanted to comply with tradition they would have brought Nadia and the baby into Taiz for forty days, so that Nadia could rest and Mum could look after them both, rather than preventing Mum from seeing her.

In reality, no woman in a village like Ashube would have been given forty days off at any time. Usually, a woman who had given birth would be carrying water, cooking, cleaning and even working in the fields within a couple of days. I remember all too well how quickly I was expected to get back to work after having Marcus. And the men would be demanding their conjugal rights immediately, regardless of any pain which the woman might be suffering. Perhaps amongst better-off Muslims the tradition still survives, but I knew that Nadia wouldn't be enjoying it.

Even though she knew the officials were lying, Mum couldn't argue with them. They simply brushed aside her protests, dismissing her as a foolish foreign woman who did not understand Muslim ways. If that was what they said was happening, all she could do was extend her visa yet again – which proved to be a terrible problem.

Faisal didn't actually believe that she would be able to get the necessary stamp. He thought that by making her wait forty days he had beaten her and she would be forced to return home without seeing Nadia again. But, through sheer good luck, Mum met a taxi driver who knew exactly where to take her to get her passport stamped to extend her visa. She would still be there when the forty days were up. Faisal was furious but could do nothing about it. He must have wondered if he would ever be rid of her.

During the forty tedious days that she had to wait around in the dust, heat and noise of Taiz, Mum met a young Syrian called Abdul. He was the cook in a restaurant that she and Jana discovered while they were staying in a hotel where the food either didn't arrive or was inedible when it did turn up.

Abdul was kind and attentive to Mum, despite the fact that anyone seen associating with a foreign woman in public was likely to get into trouble with the authorities, especially if she was a woman who had a reputation as a troublemaker. At first Mum thought he was just being friendly, until he kissed her in the middle of the restaurant. It was an incredibly brave thing for an Arab man to do in that part of the world and it was not long before the two of them had fallen in love.

I realised something was up when I was talking to her on the phone one day. I don't think anyone thinks of their parents as having any sort of romantic life, and I was probably a bit slow on the uptake. When the penny finally dropped, however, I immediately felt a terrible panic gripping me. I didn't know anything about Abdul personally, but I knew a lot about Arab men in general and how they behave towards their women. I went completely mad. I shouted at her not to do it, not to get involved. I told her that she was being stupid, that it might be a trick or he might be a spy sent by Faisal. The thought of letting another Arab man get close to our family horrified me. After all my experiences I simply couldn't imagine that he could be a genuine friend. I thought he must have an ulterior motive. There had to be an alternative explanation.

I should have known better. Mum is not someone to be put off doing what she has set her mind to, and it was none of my business anyway. Quite rightly, she took no notice of me. Mum, Jana and Abdul went to Aden to get a break from Taiz while they waited for the forty days to end.

Apparently, Jana was reluctant to go at first. She feared that she would be playing gooseberry to the young lovers, but Mum insisted. Jana spent a lot of time on her own during that little holiday, bobbing about in the sea, or sitting on the beach and reading books. I believe she and Mum needed a break from one another's company by then. They had been living practically in each other's pockets for two months. To be able to exist in a hotel room together, virtually twenty-four hours a day, is a true test of friendship.

Once I had calmed down and thought about it, I decided that, as long as Abdul was a good man, the relationship was good news. I felt that Mum deserved to have some luck. However much love and support she might get from her kids and from friends like Jana, it was never the same as having a kind and supportive partner – someone who would still be there for her when the rest of us had gone home. I knew how important Paul was in helping me to keep my sanity when everything else in the world seemed to be against me. I couldn't begrudge Mum the same comfort. She really hadn't had any life of her own since she first met Dad when she was seventeen years old and began having his children.

Whenever she mentioned Abdul, it was obvious that she was very taken with him. It must have been flattering for her to have someone interested in her again. She later told me that it was the first time she felt she had truly fallen in love. It made her feel all the sadder for Nadia, who was trapped in a loveless marriage, weighed down with children and poor health and with no apparent hope of ever escaping before she was an old woman. Neither Mum nor I are able to enjoy many of the pleasures in life without experiencing painful twinges of guilt when we remember where Nadia is and what she is having to go through.

Mum and Abdul married in Taiz, with Jana, a taxi driver and a friend of Abdul's as witnesses. I was aware that having an Arab as a husband would help Mum when she had to deal with Faisal, Mohammed and other Arab men. All of them would be more respectful of another man.

During the forty-day wait for Nadia, Mum and Jana discovered that they had been under surveillance from the moment they had arrived in the country. Many in the ex-pat community had secretly read smuggled copies of *Sold*. They knew a great deal about Nadia's plight, but all the ex-pats had been warned against having anything to do with us. Nevertheless, several of them tipped off Mum and Jana about the danger they were in.

Those who knew how the government and police worked warned Mum and Jana that there was a possibility they would be shot if they were not careful about where they went and whom they allowed to get close to them. Only a few of the bravest were willing to spend any time with them. A large percentage of the population had been told that they were wicked women trying to kidnap an innocent Yemeni wife from her loving husband. Mum and Jana found themselves almost completely isolated.

Any tape that Nadia or I had ever been forced to make — saying we were all right and loved our husbands — was played to the public or written about in the local newspapers. In every piece of propaganda Mum was characterised as being an interfering mother-in-law, intent on making her son-in-law's life a misery.

As a result every married man in Yemen hated her and everything she stood for. If one of them had come across Mum in a quiet street and had slid a dagger into her heart, it was unlikely that he would ever have been brought to justice. In fact, he would probably have been hailed as something of a hero, saving his fellow Muslim men from the terrible fate of female domination.

Many of these same men liked coming to visit the West, and even liked to live there when they could, but none of them wanted their women to become infected with the idea that they might have rights. They didn't want them to find out that they could argue with the men and possibly even get custody of their precious children; that they could choose their own clothes and handle their own money; that they could make choices about how they brought up their children or what jobs they wanted to do.

They all wanted Mum silenced. To them she was a carrier of the disease of freedom.

I had known all the risks before Mum and Jana left England, but that did not make it any easier to bear the tension of not knowing what was going on. As I waited at home for their return, my mind would conjure up horrible pictures. I could imagine a thousand different ways in which Mum could disappear and never be found again. There could be a tragic car crash, or an accident down the side of a mountain. She could be the victim of an unexplained robbery, or a mysterious attack of food poisoning. Or she might simply vanish one day, with no explanation and no clues as to what might have befallen her.

If any of these things happened I could picture the British embassy and the Foreign Office officials making all the right noises: lodging all the right complaints, expressing regret and sympathy, and promising faithfully to get to the bottom of it. I could also imagine how they would soon grow tired of pursuing the leads which would inevitably lead to dead ends. I could imagine how they would start to become irritated if our family continued to demand the truth. I could imagine how we would find it harder and harder to get responses and would eventually be treated as nuisances. The files would then be closed with sighs of relief.

They would be able to say that they had warned Mum over and over again of the dangers of the path she was following. They could tell themselves that their consciences were clear.

They had done their best, but ultimately it had all been beyond their control. If only Mum and I had been willing to accept the inevitable, they would say, this tragedy could have been avoided. But if we accepted what had happened to us as inevitable, how would things ever change? What would stop men from continuing to sell their daughters into slavery?

My imaginings haunted both my waking and sleeping hours. I found it hard to concentrate on anything and my mind was still racing whenever I went to sleep, turning waking worries into terrible nightmares. I wished Mum was safely back in England. I didn't want to lose her as well as Nadia and Marcus and have to continue the fight on my own.

After the forty days were up, the meeting with Nadia still didn't happen. More promises were broken and endless lies were told. Faisal must have been having trouble explaining to the Governor why he hadn't managed to sort out the situation and why Mum and Jana were still in the city making trouble. Faisal continued to try to bluff and worm his way out of trouble.

It didn't look as if the authorities would ever actually do as they promised as long as Mum and Jana were sitting in their hotel waiting for something to be organised. Eventually they decided to play the authorities at their own game and hatched a plan. They decided that Jana should fly out of Sana'a, telling everyone that she was going to meet me in Paris and that we would appear together on *Sacrée Soirée* to tell the world what had been happening in Taiz.

Mum was to appear to be on her way home as well. Faisal would then in all likelihood bring Nadia to Taiz and claim that Mum had just missed her. Mum could then rush back from Sana'a to see Nadia.

Sure enough, the moment Faisal thought Mum was on her way out of the country, Nadia was brought back to Taiz with the new baby. Faisal said how sad it was that Mum had not stayed a little longer. Mum immediately returned to Taiz and Faisal was unable to claim that Nadia wasn't there.

Mum and Abdul went to meet Nadia at Faisal's office with the British consul. They were allowed to spend half an hour together in a conference room. In the three months that she had been in the country Mum managed to spend only an hour in private with Nadia.

In Faisal's office she knew that there was no time to waste. Once they were alone she immediately started to plead with Nadia to come back to England. Nadia told her that she couldn't, that Mohammed had told her he would throw her out and keep the children if she even so much as mentioned going to England again.

I could imagine exactly how frightening those scenes between them would be. A man like Mohammed would be able to do whatever he wanted to his wife in the privacy of his own home and no one would intervene on her behalf. Part of me would have liked to call his bluff and have him throw Nadia out so that at least we would have her, even if we didn't have the children. But I knew that she would never be happy if it happened like that. We had to find a way to get the children free as well.

When Nadia took off her veil Mum was shocked by how ill she looked. 'Do you want to come home?' she kept asking.

'Yes, Mum. I want to come, but he won't. He won't!'

When they were no longer alone, Mum asked if Abdul could talk to Mohammed, man to man. He was now Nadia's stepfather and that would give him some negotiating power. But after the men had talked for a while, Abdul reported that Mohammed was saying Nadia would never be allowed to go to England.

Mum asked if he wanted money or a house. She said we would give him whatever he asked for. We had started to build up quite a bit of money from the book by then: we had already paid for Mum's visit to the Yemen out of it, and if I could have used the rest to buy Nadia's freedom I would have. Mum knew that when she asked the question.

Mohammed became furious at the suggestion, as if Mum had affronted his pride. He said he had a house and he did not want our money. He commanded Nadia to tell the British consul that she didn't want to go to England.

Nadia looked terrified. Mum was sure she was going to obey and for a moment she thought she was going to collapse from the emotional strain of the confrontation. After waiting so long, the pressure of actually being in a room with Nadia, knowing that she could be spirited away again at any moment should her husband decide that he had had enough, was stretching her nerves to breaking point.

'I don't want to come here any more,' Nadia said, refusing to actually say that she didn't want to come to England. Mohammed, furious at being disobeyed, ordered her to come with him. Mum watched as Nadia limped out, two paces behind her husband like a beaten dog. She knew that she would not be able to arrange another meeting now.

Unable to simply let her go without saying goodbye, Mum followed them outside. Nadia was walking towards the jeep and Mohammed was shouting angrily at her. As Mum came up to her Nadia closed her eyes and sighed.

'If you speak on French TV, Mum,' she said quietly, 'I have to phone the programme and tell them I don't want to go home.' She looked straight into Mum's eyes. 'It's not me Mum. It's the Islam. I am a Muslim. I can't come home with you. He said he will bring me, but it's not up to me if I can come home or not. It's up to him. I want to come home, but . . .'

'I love you Nard,' Mum said, not wanting to put her through any more pain, and they hugged. Mum held her close, showering her with kisses, feeling Nadia's frail body shaking with silent sobs. Any mother will be able to imagine how that must have been for Mum, how helpless she must have felt and how close to total despair.

5

The Foreign Office

Our already tense relations with the Foreign Office were not improved by Mum's visit to Yemen. Because she had not expected to stay for so long, Mum ran out of money after the first couple of weeks. She contacted me asking me to send her some more. I was more than happy to do this. The book was starting to earn good royalties, and I saw the money as being part of a pot for the fight for Nadia. Having Mum actually in Yemen seemed like the best chance we had of getting to Nadia. I would have paid whatever was necessary to improve her chances.

I knew nothing about moving money around from country to country, however, and I had to find someone to help me.

When Mum had asked for money before, I got it to her via an official in the Foreign Office in London. I had simply telephoned, and it had been arranged for the money to go to the embassy in Sana'a.

97

As soon as Mum told me she was going to have to stay another forty days I made a phone call. As soon as I said who I was, I faced a hostile tone. I explained the problem and asked if they would help as they had before.

'What is wrong with you people?' I was asked. 'Nadia is all right where she is. I'm not sending any more money. I've already helped you once. I'm not doing it again.' The phone was slammed down, leaving me feeling angry and helpless. Those aggressive words burned into my brain. I hurled the phone across the room, smashing it to pieces. The fury that had been boiling inside me for years exploded.

It was as if a light had been switched on in my brain. 'You people.' I felt that was a reference to the colour of my skin. In that moment I became convinced that part of our problem was a racial one. If Nadia and I had had two wholly white parents there would never have been any question of us having 'dual nationality'. No one would have questioned for a moment that it was wrong for us to be sold into marriage, imprisoned in Mokbana against our will and raped. Nadia was legally a minor by British law when she was forced to the marriage bed. If our name had been Smith and we had been blonde and blue-eyed, we would have been out of those mountains within months, or even weeks.

Other events have confirmed this for me since. When two English girls were convicted of smuggling drugs in Bangkok, John Major was immediately on to their case, demanding that they be freed from prison and sent back to England. They had actually committed a crime but the Prime Minister was willing to wade in and do deals on their behalf. When we heard how the girls were being brought home, Mum sent John Major a letter, saying how disgusted she was that her daughters had never been given such assistance, but she never received a reply.

When two British nurses were found guilty of murder in Saudi Arabia and imprisoned, the politicians went to work again and these women were back in Britain in no time. We were imprisoned in a Muslim country just like them, but we had committed no crime. We were the victims of other people's crimes, but no ministers came to our rescue. No one with the power to make things happen demanded that we should have justice.

When Yemeni tribesmen kidnapped some European tourists the international outcry was immediate.

The only difference that I can see between us and the others was the colour of our skins. Conversations like the one with the Foreign Office official made me feel so angry I was lost for words.

The British government have also been completely inconsistent in their policy towards child brides in the Yemen. When a fifteen-year-old girl called Aisha was recently taken from Wales in exactly the same way as Nadia and I were, her MP rang Mum for advice. He told her that Aisha's mother was in a terrible state.

'Tell her not to give up,' Mum said. 'Tell her to write to the Foreign Office to tell them what has happened. But warn her that they will say there is nothing they can do because she is a dual national.'

'She has already done that and that is exactly what the

Foreign Office said,' the MP told her. 'But they are still willing to try to get her out.'

'Wish her luck,' Mum said. 'We managed it with Zana, but only after eight years.'

There was then a lot of press coverage of the case and the next we heard was that the British diplomatic staff in Yemen had snatched Aisha and held her in the embassy over there until she could be flown back to Wales. The British government had done for her exactly what they should have done for us in 1980.

We were thrilled for her, obviously, and hoped that it might mean there had been a change of policy which would mean that we would stand a better chance of getting Nadia back but it didn't happen. It seemed that Aisha's family had been lucky in the choice of the person they asked for help. He had succeeded in working a miracle which everyone else had told us was impossible.

Although we feel angry that we have not been treated in the same way, Aisha's case does at least hold up the hope to us that if we can just find the right person to fight for our cause we will be able to get what we want. But how do we find that person?

When the civil war between the north and the south of Yemen started, and bombs were being dropped on Aden, the Foreign Office started to evacuate all British citizens from the area, regardless of whether they had the right papers. We became desperate. Now, on top of everything else, Nadia was going to be at the centre of a war zone – as if she hadn't been through enough! We hoped this would prove to be a blessing in disguise, providing us with a new way out. Mum rang the Foreign Office to ask if they could get Nadia and the children out along with the other Brits.

'We have no intention of bringing Nadia out of Yemen,' came the reply. It seemed that their minds were made up. Because they did not act quickly enough at the beginning of our imprisonment, Nadia had become trapped. In their eyes she had now been there so long that there was nothing they could do about it. They were washing their hands of her.

As far as the Foreign Office were concerned, Nadia could be sick but they would not help to cure her. She could be in danger of being killed and they would not be willing to even try to help her get out. She could be forced to bear children for her husband until her body finally gave up, it was not the Foreign Office's business.

Over the years the British government have changed their story so many times that it is hard to remember what they were saying at the beginning. They now claim that I signed a letter to the British embassy in 1980 asking for a visa for my husband to visit England. I have no memory of any such letter, but then I was a traumatised fifteen-year-old and would probably have signed anything that Abdul Khada, my so-called father-in-law, told me to sign.

I have never seen this letter but, if it exists, the authorities say that it proves that our marriages were just marriages of convenience, arranged for the boys to get British passports.

If that is true, it certainly wasn't my idea, nor was it Nadia's. We were not in a position to cook up any such plan, and never would have done. We didn't know the boys or their families until we got to Yemen. Why would we want to marry them in order to get them to England? If it was a marriage of 'convenience' we certainly did not profit. We were just pawns in other people's games. Yet Dad, Gowad and Abdul Khada, all the people who schemed against us, lived happily in England while Nadia remained an exile.

Whenever we actually get to see an official face to face, they always see our point. They agree that it is a scandal which must be put right. But it always ends the same way, in silence or in an official letter disclaiming all responsibility.

It was becoming clearer and clearer to us that we were on our own. We could not rely on our country to help us.

All through the three months that she was in Yemen, Mum was aware that Gerald Ryan, the British Consul, was on edge. We knew that we were a constant thorn in his side and that just having Mum in the country would have made his job harder, but it was more than that. Something was going on at the embassy which appeared to implicate him.

Mum and Jana heard rumours amongst the expatriate community about possible corruption, but didn't take much notice. To be honest, the idea that there might be corruption in the system did not come as a surprise to any of us. We knew from the way in which we had been treated in the past that there must be people bringing undue influence to bear on the officials all the time. There were too many coincidences, and information always seemed to leak out to someone who shouldn't have it.

We didn't know whether that meant people were being

threatened or bribed, or whether they were simply protecting some vested interests. We just knew that we never seemed to receive any straight talk from anyone. Yemen has a culture in which the giving and receiving of favours amongst men is taken for granted. I feel that the people working in the embassy were perhaps no different from those they worked amongst.

There were auditors looking at the embassy's books on several occasions when Mum and Jana were in the building trying to see people, and it was obvious that Ryan was nervous about what they might find. Because Mum was only interested in one thing, getting to see Nadia, she paid virtually no attention to what else might have been going on. It wasn't until a few years later that we discovered what was actually happening in the back offices of that embassy while the officials were putting on a brave face to the outside world.

Once, when she was in Ryan's office, the embassy security guards came up to say that there was a man downstairs wanting to see him, who was refusing to be searched. Ryan asked who he was and they said some Arabic name. 'Oh that's all right,' Ryan brushed their worries aside. 'Let him in.'

'How come?' Mum and Jana asked, surprised by such a casual attitude to security in a country where many men carry guns as a matter of course.

'Oh, it's OK,' he said. 'We do things for them and they do things for us. It's the way it's done.'

Mum and Jana began to feel very uncomfortable about their own safety in Ryan's care.

The information Mum was getting was totally contradictory. During another of her visits to Ryan, he told her that there had been a court case in Taiz in which Nadia's and my marriages were declared illegal. It was the first any of us had heard of this, and it made no sense to us. Mum asked him if he could find documentary evidence and he said he would. Needless to say, he never did, but he did come up with a piece of paper which stated that Abdullah had remarried me after I had left for England. We knew nothing about that either.

If I had gone to the village, as Chawki had tried to persuade me to do, when we went to see Nadia with the French film crew, the men could have kept me there. They could have used this piece of paper as justification for their actions, saying that I was still Abdullah's wife and therefore a Yemeni citizen, and the whole thing would have started all over again. My blood runs cold when I think what might have happened to me on that trip.

Although we were constantly becoming discouraged about our efforts to save Nadia, we never gave up trying for long. Keeping in contact with the embassy in Sana'a was one of our best chances of hearing if anything was changing in Mokbana. But we could tell that things there were going from bad to worse. Every time we rang them up we found ourselves being put through to a new person. We would then be told they were 'not familiar with our case', and we would have to explain our story all over again.

The new voice would nearly always be shocked by what they heard and would say that something would have to be done. They would say that they would have to go off and 'look up our files' or 'talk to a colleague'. We would then be left with a mixture of hopefulness and despair.

Everyone was always promising to 'get back to us', but they never did. A few weeks or months later, when we had to accept that the promised call was not going to materialise, we would ring again and the whole process would be repeated. It was horribly depressing.

We knew from all our dealings with the embassy in Sana'a that it was never run as it should have been. There was always an air of shiftiness about the place, of half-truths being told and of alliances which were never spoken about but which changed the way things were being done behind the scenes. Gerald Ryan, the consul, left Sana'a rather hurriedly in June 1993. We were used to people doing that.

Then we heard that the investigators who had been there during Mum's visit had found some 'irregularities' in the finances at the embassy. As the extent of these irregularities became known we heard in February 1994 that Ryan had been arrested. The following December we heard that he had hanged himself.

The British government then decided it was time to investigate these 'irregularities' in more depth. If someone as eminent as a British consul was prepared to kill himself rather than face the consequences of whatever had been going on, they had better find out more about it. We followed their investigations as closely as we could. Whenever we were speaking to anyone, we would ask questions and we got hold of any reports that were issued. The picture began to piece together like a jigsaw, but there were still some vital pieces missing.

In 1995 the Committee of Public Accounts produced a

report which catalogued some of what had been going on. It was a very formal document, taking two paragraphs to say what could have been said in a sentence, embellishing everything with legal jargon to cover every eventuality. But even their fancy language couldn't disguise the fact that the investigators were shocked by what they had found.

They admitted that there had been inadequate controls of how the embassy money was handled. The Committee were astonished to find that the staff at the embassy had been allowed to use public money to speculate on the local currency market, making a profit for themselves of £670,000 in a relatively short period.

There were examples quoted in the report of inflated prices being agreed with contractors who gave Ryan bribes.

We could imagine just how the system had worked. If a building job needed doing on an embassy property, the builder who offered Ryan or some other official the biggest bribe would get the job – regardless of whether they had quoted the lowest rate or were the best equipped to do the work. This sort of business practice may have been quite normal in Yemen, but it was not the sort of practice from which British officials should have been profiting.

The investigators also discovered that Ryan had negotiated a five-year lease on the ambassador's residence which made him a personal gain of US $50,000 in the form of a bribe which he kept for himself.

On top of that, the report said that the Foreign Office had neglected to tell the investigators that another government department, Overseas Development Administration, were investigating the possibility of more irregularities at the embassy. They too had been looking into the misuse of their funds during the same period. (No wonder things had got too hot for Ryan.) Two separate investigations were going on and he had been trying to keep one from knowing about the other.

Ryan couldn't have made his scams work on his own. He needed to recruit others. He was able to do this because there were no job specifications for locally engaged staff. Ryan recruited friends to key positions, rather than going out to look for the best people for the jobs. As a result, many of the staff were under a personal obligation to him and could easily be put under pressure should he want certain transactions to go through without the full range of checks being made.

The report explained how the staff had managed to make big personal profits with embassy money. Apparently, local currency would be drawn from the embassy's sterling account at the official exchange rates in order to pay a bill. Some of the money was then converted at the black market rates, which could be up to four times higher, to pay whatever bill was outstanding. The difference was pocketed by Ryan and an accomplice. Profiteering was possible because of the many different exchange rates which were available.

The investigators were also concerned at the mishandling of visa applications. Sometimes applicants were not interviewed or were not asked to fill out the relevant forms. Some people who should not have been given the right to enter Britain could easily have gained visas as a result. No doubt many did. This made us feel all the more bitter. The people who made virtually no effort to help Nadia and her children out of the country were helping those who were willing to bribe them. Perhaps we would have made them an offer as well during the short time that we had the money if we had known more about the way the system worked.

The ambassador to the Yemen at the time that Ryan was consul was condemned by the report for being guilty of appalling mismanagement. The investigators questioned whether he should have received the pension he did or the compensation payment of £23,000 given to him for leaving the job.

A year and a half later, after a new ambassador had arrived, an internal audit found it necessary to make over 150 recommendations for improvements to controls. There was a civil war going on in Yemen at the time and, given the mess that the Sana'a post was in, the investigators didn't think that the Foreign Office had appointed a man with sufficient management capability or given him enough incentive to sort out the mess. Instead, the report accused them of allowing the situation to deteriorate to a point at which they found it necessary to give early retirement to their replacement ambassador.

The investigators were appalled that the Foreign Office did nothing though they knew about the poor level of management.

Having experienced the way the embassy worked at first hand, we didn't think any of these findings were very surprising. In a way we were relieved to see that we had not been imagining things and that an official investigation bore out many of the things which we had been saying were wrong.

The Foreign Office repeatedly gave us the impression that they would much rather do nothing. They allowed a situation to deteriorate rather than make an effort to clear it up quickly. It was because of this indifference that little was done to get Nadia and me out of Yemen when we were still children, before we had children of our own. Instead they have allowed the situation to deteriorate to a stage where they now have a woman in her thirties with six children who wants to get out instead of two enslaved children.

Ryan had a French wife living in the Yemen with him, but also had a mistress whom he employed at the embassy for a month and sent to interview Nadia.

The mistress reported back to Ryan that Nadia had said she wanted to stay in Yemen. He went to see Nadia himself and wrote a report of the meeting. In it he claimed that Nadia said she wanted to have the whole matter dropped because of the publicity. But Ryan admitted that both Mohammed and Faisal Abdul Aziz were in the room throughout the interview, so Nadia would not have been able to say what she truly felt. He said that Nadia looked 'frightened' and was 'undoubtedly intimidated'. Despite this description of her state of mind, the Foreign Office was still happy to use the report by quoting Nadia's words as if she had said them of her own free will. They made it sound as if her words settled the matter once and for all.

I knew Faisal Abdul Aziz from the period when I was still trapped in Yemen, and I had heard a lot more about his methods of intimidation from Mum and Jana. He told me when they allowed me to leave that they were letting me go because

I was 'trouble' and that Nadia was to stay because she was their 'insurance policy'. He always ensured that Nadia was never alone when meeting representatives of the British embassy, or Mum or me. I could imagine just what he would have been saying to Nadia before Ryan turned up that day. That, coupled with threats from Mohammed, would have been more than enough to send Nadia into the robot-like state we had all seen before, spouting the approved lines.

While people we meet from the Foreign Office often sound sympathetic at a personal level, as soon as they begin to act officially they immediately stop wanting to become involved. The official line appeared to be that we were not to be helped. One acting ambassador actually told Mum that he had been instructed by the Foreign Office not to give us assistance.

It is as if everyone who hears our story for the first time responds as a human being and wants to help. They go to the files and they see how long it has been dragging on and what a mess their predecessors have made of it. They then worry that if they commit themselves to helping it will be an enormous amount of work and the chances are they will fail and have that failure on their career record. They check with a superior who tells them to drop it. They immediately attempt to pass the buck to someone more junior or they try to talk us into giving up.

We only find these things out because Mum refuses to give up. She just keeps on asking questions, insisting that justice is not being served and trying to discover the truth. Slowly but surely, step by step, she is getting closer to unravelling just why our case has been going so wrong for us for so many years. It is certain that the embassy in Sana'a and the Foreign Office both played significant parts in the mystery and have to bear their share of responsibility for Nadia's suffering.

6

Rescue?

Twenty years ago we were totally naïve, with complete faith in our country. We imagined that as soon as the Foreign Office discovered our plight they would rescue us. For a long while we listened to their excuses and explanations and accepted them. Gradually we became more sceptical. Now we believe that there are so many layers of deceit, so many people with hidden agendas, perhaps with careers and pensions to protect, and so much laziness that looking after British citizens was the smallest of their worries. It was impossible for us ever to know exactly who was in a position to help, who was using us for their own financial or political gains and who was simply trying to fob us off in the hope that we would give up and go away.

Mum now has files and files of letters and documents which show what a tangled web has been spun around us over the years. We are by no means the only family to find ourselves in this position, but the vast majority of mothers have given up fighting because there seemed to be no way for them to get past the bureaucrats, lawyers and politicians. Few could have fought as long and hard as my mum has. For her, the nightmare began more than thirty years ago.

Nadia and I have an elder brother and sister, Laila and Ahmed. Dad took them out to the Yemen to visit his family in Aden when they were very small. Mum had just given birth to Nadia and had had a very hard time. Dad told her that he would give her a break by going away for a while and taking the two bigger children with him.

It was Christmas time and Dad had sold our house to pay for the trip, leaving us in a rented room. Mum had no money at all and had to give us jam sandwiches on Christmas Day. Obviously, Nadia and I were too young to know the difference, but it must have been a bleak time for Mum. She loved us, but she was beginning to think that she might have made a mistake in starting a family with my dad. Nevertheless, she looked forward to his return and to getting back her two older children.

But when Dad returned everything had changed. Mum discovered that he had left Laila and Ahmed with his parents. At first he said they were just staying on for a bit longer because they were having such a good time. Eventually he admitted that they weren't coming back. He claimed that he wanted them to be brought up as good Muslims. He didn't want them to be subjected to the temptations of the West. When Nadia and I went to Yemen in 1980 we met them for the first time. Laila was eighteen and was already married. Ahmed, at seventeen, was in the army.

The most extraordinary thing about the way Dad has treated all of us is that he had suffered the same fate when he was a child. He knew how terrible enforced marriages could be and yet he was still able to inflict them on his children. When he first came to England and met Mum he was escaping from an arranged marriage in Aden. He had been fifteen years old and his wife had been even younger. He told Mum that the marriage had never been consummated and that he had had to come to England in order to earn a living. He also told her that after meeting her he had arranged a divorce. We do not know if this is true. Whatever the case, his first wife died many years ago and – unbelievable as it may seem, when you think about what he was able to get away with – he never married Mum.

Now that I have children of my own I can imagine how Mum must have felt that day when she went to the door to greet Dad. She expected to sweep her children up into her arms and listen to their excited chatter about their wonderful holiday, only to find that they had vanished and the man she loved had betrayed her in the most terrible way. Something must have died inside her that day.

I sometimes wonder why she didn't fight to get Laila and Ahmed back as she did for Nadia and me, but I guess she was too young and too inexperienced. She also had two babies to look after and it wasn't long before she was pregnant again. Dad later told her, in a drunken fit of temper, that he kept her pregnant through all those years in order to keep control of her. I imagine that is true. It seems to be exactly what is now happening to Nadia.

Since I escaped from Yemen, both Laila and Ahmed have returned to England and they have stayed. Laila's children are now completely English. It is as if she had never been away.

In a way it gives me hope that if Laila was able to return after so many years, Nadia should be able to as well. At the same time I feel a deep resentment. Why are they allowed to travel freely when she isn't? Why is she the only one living in Yemen when all her brothers and sisters are now free and living in England? I can see no sense in it, find no justice. It all seems so arbitrary and cruel.

I do not feel close to either Laila or Ahmed. We maintain a family relationship, but I know that anything I say to them could be repeated back to Dad. I keep off personal subjects. Neither of them makes any effort to visit Mum. They were very young when Dad took them away and they never had a chance to bond with her.

I suppose the same thing might happen if Marcus ever comes to England as a young man. Will he blame me for leaving him? Will he ever understand why I decided to come out when I did? Will his father's family have poisoned his mind against me? What stories will he have been told about his terrible English mother? Will he feel the same way towards women as his father and grandfather do? I suppose it is inevitable that he will have many of the same attitudes as the men he has been brought up amongst. That makes me feel very sad.

I wonder sometimes who he would have had to be a mother to him after I left. Perhaps Ward, his grandmother, took him under her wing. I know she hated me, but I hope she didn't take it out on him when he was so little and so frightened and confused by what was happening all around him. He was such a tiny, helpless creature when I left him. But maybe Ward would have been sympathetic about his frailty. After all, his father had been just the same way and she had cared for him. I can only hope that once I was out of the way she took pity on her little grandson.

When Mum, Jana and Mum's new husband, Abdul, got back to England a huge weight lifted from my shoulders. Although I was horribly disappointed that Mum hadn't managed to free Nadia, at least she had survived the ordeal herself. I had truly begun to fear that I would never see her again.

I felt very nervous about meeting Abdul, our new stepfather. I couldn't imagine that, in my current frame of mind, I was likely to take to any Arab man, particularly one who had managed to work his way into the family. To my great relief we all liked him. Thinking back, he must have been more nervous than us, coming to a strange country and meeting a whole new, grown-up family. I dare say Mum had warned him how snappy and bad-tempered I could be. I later discovered that he was quite scared of me. If he knew I was coming round, he would tell Mum he was going upstairs and wouldn't reappear until I had gone. I think perhaps he felt uncomfortable because he knew how I felt about Arab men in general due to the way we had been treated. It must have been hard for him trying to find his place as Mum's husband when we were around the house so much.

Abdul is a quiet, hard-working man, very different from

Dad and from the men in Gowad and Abdul Khada's families. He did not attempt to play the heavy father to any of us and he showed that he intended to work hard to make something of his life. He passed his driving test and went to college to study English and get some certificates. He got work as a chef. We were all very happy for Mum. She obviously found his company and support a great help.

Although we were all getting on with our lives as best we could, the shadow of Nadia's continued imprisonment was always looming in the backs of our minds. Mum continued to contact every official source she could think of, nagging everyone she came across. But in our hearts we knew that if we wanted to get Nadia out, we were going to have to do it ourselves. I concentrated my efforts on publicising *Sold*, hoping that if I talked to enough journalists our story would eventually reach the right ears.

We were swimming around like innocents in a shark pool, hoping that each new person we came across would be the one who would provide the help we needed. We wanted to get Nadia back so much. We were willing to believe any promises anyone made to us, and to pay any amount of money to make it possible.

I first heard about a military-style organisation which claimed to specialise in rescuing lost children in 1992. I was in Sweden having lunch with my publisher during a publicity tour.

I had become very used to travelling around Europe in the previous eighteen months or so. Going to Rome, Stockholm or Amsterdam was no different to going down to London. I was as comfortable in airports as I was in train stations. It seemed like a million years since I had set out from Heathrow Airport on that first terrible adventure in 1980, but it was only twelve years. Then I had no idea what to expect when I stepped inside a plane, now I saw them as glorified buses to get me from one appointment to the next.

Mostly I travelled back and forth to Paris, where the book had sold over a million copies and the publishers were always wanting me to give another interview to a journalist or appear on another television show. All the publicity surrounding the *Sacrée Soirée* programmes had made my face and my story famous in France, and the French people in the street made me feel like I was one of them. They were always concerned and interested to find out what was happening in our lives.

On the first few trips I was terrified at the thought of being in a strange foreign city, where nobody would be able to understand a word I said and I wouldn't even know how to ask for a cup of coffee or a toilet. To begin with I stayed in the hotel rooms all the time with Mum, or whichever friend or relative I was travelling with. Unless the publishers supplied someone to show me around and take care of all the practical arrangements, I didn't have the nerve even to walk out into the hotel corridor on my own.

Eventually, however, when they had me there for days on end, I had to pluck up the courage to go out on my own or go mad. I couldn't sit inside a hotel room day after day, knowing that one of the greatest cities in the world was just outside the front door.

Stepping out into the street without an escort was a huge

breakthrough for me. I suddenly discovered that I could do it, that I was free to do whatever I wanted. Perhaps, in my mind, I still had the feeling that I should be behind closed doors, or covered in veils. I had spent eight years fighting the idea that I should be invisible and should never act on my own initiative. Some of the brainwashing must have got through to me.

I had been full of self-confidence before I left Birmingham, quite happy to move around the city between friends' houses, school and the youth club. All that self-confidence had been trained out of me in Mokbana and now I had to rediscover it and allow it to mature.

Once I had broken through the barrier I found that I loved Paris. I soon grew to know my way around the streets of the romantic capital of the world as well as I knew my native Birmingham. Sometimes I would go there two or three times in a week, just flying in to do one interview and then forgetting something I had wanted to say and going back again a few days later.

I often took two-year-old Liam with me, hating to be apart from him more than I had to be, and wanting him to share some of the excitement of flying and travelling while it was on offer. The publishers became used to having him rushing around their offices, getting into everything and distracting the grown-ups from their work.

At the immigration desks at Charles de Gaulle Airport they never even bothered to stop me and look at my passport any more.

'Hi, Zana,' the officials would say with a casual wave, 'enjoy your trip.'

It was a good feeling, realising that so many people knew about us and cared what happened to us, but it was a strain too. The trips weren't just about wandering around the streets looking at the sights. On some of them I would have no free time at all. Instead, I would be cooped up in a hotel room talking to the media from the moment I got off the plane to the moment I rushed back on to it. Everything would be run to a tight schedule. Journalists would be brought to the room every half-hour, or every hour if they were important enough, and I would have to answer all the same questions over and over again, reliving all the horrors that I had gone through so many times before.

I was happy to do it, however tiring and emotionally stressful it might be, because I knew that every time the story was retold the chances increased that someone in power would hear about Nadia's plight and come to our rescue. Every piece of editorial that appeared to embarrass the Yemeni government increased our chances of something being done, or so I thought.

I also enjoyed the adventure side of the travelling. I loved seeing new sights and meeting new people. I loved trying different foods and finding out about different people's lives. I was hungry for information and experiences. It was as if I was making up for the years I had lost.

Every new experience gave me more strength for the fight ahead. It was shaping me into the person I have become. At the same time, I felt guilty too. Here I was, able to hop on and off planes, being taken around wonderful cities and treated like a VIP, while Nadia was still stuck in Mokbana. Knowing that she should have been there with me took away much of the pleasure of being a young girl who had accidentally written a bestseller.

I discovered later that the Yemeni authorities told Nadia and Mohammed that I had done it all for the money. That was never true. I never gave the money a second thought.

I hate to think how Nadia must have felt when she heard this. No doubt everything she was told was exaggerated in order to make her feel that I had abandoned her and was cynically cashing in on her misery. I just hope that deep inside she understood. She knew that for the first twenty-two years of her life I fought to protect her in every way I could. Hopefully she didn't believe them when they told her I had given up on her. I know in bad moments she says she believes we've forgotten her. It must feel like that when the months drag past and she hears nothing, but I hope she never thinks in her heart that we will ever give up fighting for her.

When I left her in 1988 I promised that I would get her out straight away. I hope that she will one day know how hard I have worked to keep that promise.

I still feel that guilt today. Whenever I am offered some new experience I immediately feel bad because Nadia can't do it with me. My first instinct is to turn down anything that is offered. Then I have to tell myself that everything I am doing is for her. The more I learn, and the more people I meet, the better my chances of getting her free.

I know that if she had been the one to get out, and I had been left behind, then she would be doing exactly the same for me. Except that I also know that if I had been the one left behind I wouldn't be there because they would have wanted to get rid of me years ago. I would never have been as docile and obliging as Nadia is. I would have been fighting them every inch of the way, spitting and clawing at them like a rabid cat, and I feel sure that by now they would have grown tired of the battle and would have sent me home.

Everything I do I am doing for Nadia as well as for myself. It is as if we are spiritual Siamese twins and I'm incomplete because she is not with me in the flesh. In one way it feels like a permanent sort of grief, in another it is a comfort to feel that she is still part of me, even when she is so far away.

I always stay in the simplest hotels whenever I am given a choice. I don't find that I need luxury. I am not comfortable with it. On my first trip to Paris they put me into a hotel which, I guess, was one of the grandest in the city. I was flattered but very uncomfortable. I felt out of place and conspicuous. After one night I asked them to move me somewhere where I would feel more at home. They found me a simpler hotel which became my base for nearly all my future visits.

Although the promotion tours were exciting and fun, the pressure was immense. Having Liam there would sometimes add to the strain, but if he didn't come I would miss him and would want to get back to him, which was a distraction.

All the time that I talked about the book, I was reminded about Nadia. I felt we were all failing her and I would want to go into a corner and cry. But no matter how bad I felt, the relentless and repetitive questions would keep coming. I would have to go over and over the details of our lives in the villages and our battles with the authorities again and again until the words spilled out of my mouth automatically, my brain too tired to follow them.

'How does it feel to lose your sister?'

'How does it feel to leave a small child behind and never see him again?'

'Why have you written the book?'

'Do you think you will ever see them again?'

'How do you feel about your father?'

The thicker and faster the questions came, the harder I found it to think of clear answers which would explain to people how it had all happened and why it had to stop. Sometimes I would hear myself saying something I didn't mean or contradicting something I had already said because they kept on asking more questions and I was talking, talking, talking.

If it was just Mum and me and a few friends or family sitting round a table at home we would talk over every angle of our problem incessantly. If one of us lost our temper or said something stupid it didn't matter. They were like brain-storming sessions. But journalists want to be able to take your words and put them straight into print or on to the screen. They want to shape whatever material you give them into a story which is all their own. Things always become distorted when you are discussing such emotional subjects, but when you are discussing them with the media the distortions become a matter of record, and the truth becomes more unclear and muddy with each new piece of publicity.

In Stockholm that day we were taking a break from one of

these rounds of interviews. Even over meals on trips like this the conversation seldom strayed from the book and the story which we were telling the world. It was not my first trip to Stockholm and I already knew the publishers. Liam was there that day, taking up more than half my attention, and my friend Jackie was with me. The publishers were always very good about letting me bring a friend, or one of my sisters for company, if Mum couldn't make it.

'Have you seen this?' asked my publisher's secretary, passing across a book which seemed to be about some military people. There was a picture of a man in some sort of combat uniform holding a child in his arms, giving the impression that he had just saved it from someone.

'No,' I replied, glancing at it casually, one eye on Liam as he disappeared under the table again. It didn't look like the sort of book I would have any interest in. 'Why?'

'It's about a group of people – they don't like to be called mercenaries but I guess that would be the best description. They go round rescuing children for their parents, things like that.'

'What sort of rescues?' I asked. She now had almost my full attention.

'Well, if a divorced father snatches his kids and takes them off to his native country and the mother can't get them back by legal means, these guys will go in and snatch them back. That sort of thing. There are about four different stories in the book of rescues they've done. They're Americans.'

I picked the glossy book up again and flipped through the pages. I doubted if I would be able to read it myself – I never seemed to be able to concentrate on anything any more – but I wanted to know more. Before I went to Yemen I used to read a lot, but whenever I picked up a book now, Liam would be tugging on my sleeve or climbing on to my lap and my thoughts would be distracted by a hundred other things.

'Can I borrow this?' I asked. 'For my mum to look at.'

'Of course,' she said, 'it's for you to take.'

I decided I would take it back to Mum – she was always better at researching things than I was. I knew that she was still battling away at the authorities, though she spared me the details these days. She knew that I had my hands full with the book and with Liam so she tried not to worry me unnecessarily. I was grateful for that and had stopped asking her questions about what she was up to. I knew that if she had a breakthrough I would be the first to know, and I just didn't feel able to cope with all the setbacks and disappointments which I knew she must be coming up against every day.

Although I didn't know the details of what she was up to, I knew Mum wasn't coping too well with the stress either. She seemed to survive on a mixture of nicotine and adrenaline.

On the plane back to England I flicked absent-mindedly through the book while Jackie entertained Liam. There were pictures of very capable-looking military men and happy, smiling children and I thought how wonderful it would be if we could be welcoming Nadia and the children back to Birmingham, so that we could call a halt to the whole mad media circus and get on with the rest of our lives. The man in the picture exuded an air of confidence. He looked like someone who was capable of achieving whatever he set his mind to.

I fell to day-dreaming about how great it would have been if Nadia and I could have written *Sold* together. We could be travelling around together to promote it, and enjoying spending the money it was earning. But maybe if we were both safely home we would have wanted to put the whole experience behind us and get on with our private lives. Our story would have ended the day we landed at Gatwick.

I saw Mum the next day and gave her the book.

'That looks interesting,' she said, putting it aside to look at later. The seeds of our next disaster had just been sown.

We had a cup of tea and a chat and I didn't think any more about it. It was impossible to keep track of everything that was going on in the family. We all had enough to do just keeping up with our own lives. Having children does that to you. The time just seems to evaporate. My days passed in a sort of blur as I kept trying to find ways of sorting out my life.

I had moved into a nice little Housing Association flat and most of my time was taken up with looking after Liam. The money which was beginning to come in from the book was very helpful for buying things for him, but my life was really a matter of getting along from day to day. I managed to buy myself a little car, which thrilled me. It gave me the freedom I wanted to get about Birmingham and visit people.

A couple of weeks later Mum brought up the subject again. 'I read that book you gave me,' she said. 'I think we should get in touch with these people.'

'Well, you must do what you've gotta do,' I said, indifferently. I didn't think about it any more. I was becoming more philosophical about our situation. When I had first arrived back from Yemen I had become excited about every little thing that happened, determined to make everything work, impatient to get Nadia and the children out as quickly as possible. Time had taught me that there was no point in getting into a state about every promise someone made or every ray of hope that was held out. I had had so many disappointments that I no longer pinned my hopes on anything. If Mum wanted to approach these people then I would be very interested to hear what they had to say, but I wasn't going to hold my breath.

A few weeks later I was round at her house with Liam, probably having a cup of tea as usual, when she said, 'We're meeting one of those guys.'

'What guys?' My mind was miles away as I tried to stop Liam pushing something into his mouth.

'The ones in that book you gave me,' Mum said, as if it were obvious.

'Never!' I was taken by surprise.

'Yeah, we've got hold of them and they want a meeting. One of them's coming over from America.'

'What do you want me to do?' I asked.

'I'll meet him first,' she said. 'I don't want you running around the place on wild goose chases. You've got enough to do with looking after Liam at the moment. I'll let you know what he says.'

Against my better judgement, I felt a tiny flame of hope flaring up inside me once more.

Mum was told she was going to meet a woman called Judy. She flew in from America and a meeting was arranged in a service station on a motorway somewhere between London and Birmingham. It seemed a suitably bleak and anonymous venue. The sort of place where secrets could be traded without any fear of being overheard by a journalist or spotted by a nosy neighbour.

There was an air of secrecy about the whole thing which seemed appropriate for the sort of operations in which this organisation specialised. Once I heard that Mum was actually going to meet them, the little spark of hope began to grow and glow inside me. I started to become excited at the possibility that we had found a new way forward.

There had been many a night when I had dreamed of simply hiring a helicopter and swooping into the mountains of Mokbana to snatch back the missing members of my family. In the cold light of day I would remember how hard it had been for anyone to challenge the men of the villages and I realised that my dream was as much of a fantasy as a James Bond movie. That didn't stop me from dreaming of a task force of hard men, probably made up of Bruce Willis, Sylvester Stallone and Arnold Schwarzenegger, who would tell me not to worry any more and to leave everything to them.

And then this secretive group of people turned up. They had a track record in operations that was just like a movie script. Maybe my dream wasn't a fantasy after all. Maybe this was the way forward. Maybe, I told myself, our mistake up till now had been our reliance on diplomats who had careers to protect and whose whole lives were dedicated to caution, compromise and lengthy negotiation.

We knew now that diplomacy would never work. That was

obvious. We needed people who were not frightened to take some action, people who would use force if necessary to overcome the men who were holding my sister prisoner. We needed people who were willing to take some risks and who believed that the ends justified the means. People, in other words, who were ready to 'kick some ass'.

Mum was driven to the meeting by a friend and all through the afternoon I found it impossible to relax as the possibilities circled round inside my head. I tried to play with Liam but my mind kept wandering back on to what might be going on in that service station and what the Americans might be able to do for us.

The fact that they were Americans somehow made me feel even more optimistic. Not just because it made them seem more like the heroes of a blockbuster action movie but also because we had seen how the Americans had pushed Saddam Hussein out of Kuwait and had recovered their hostages from Iran. I felt that they would be less inclined to worry about damaging diplomatic relations with a Middle Eastern country. I was being illogical, of course, because these people were not the American government, but the whole idea of an American force going in for Nadia seemed feasible. I was happy to talk myself into believing that we were almost home and dry.

Despite the many disappointments and setbacks which we had suffered, I was still desperate to find some sort of fairy godmother or godfather. One who would wave a wand, take all the worry and responsibility out of our hands and promise to deliver Nadia and the kids back to me.

That evening Mum rang.

'How did it go?' I asked.

'It was good,' she said, in her usual style of dead-pan under-statement. 'We had a long chat and she's very confident that they can do this mission.'

'What do they need?' I wanted to know. 'Do they need money?'

'They haven't mentioned money yet. They need facts. They need to know what the countryside is like round the villages. They need to have it all described to them.'

'I can do that,' I said. The details of the place where I had spent those hideous eight years were still burned into my memory. I could describe every track and every rock, every scrawny tree and every barren mountain. The territory had been unmapped when we first arrived, or so everyone told Mum when she started trying to find us. But inside my head was the most detailed map imaginable. I had walked those dusty tracks every day, and been driven in and out of Taiz, dreaming of the time when I would be able to escape. I wanted to give them every piece of information that was still in my head.

Over the next few days Mum and Jana and I sat round Mum's kitchen table and did as many rough drawings and diagrams as we could. We showed just where Nadia's house was and where the other houses were in relation to it. We showed where the tracks going in and out of the village were, and where the best vantage points would be for watching the comings and goings of the men without being spotted.

I wrote down everything I could remember about the city of Taiz and the transport systems and about the road out into the

Mokbana. I listed the signposts and the villages along the way. I was becoming euphoric at being able to plan actively once more. It was so much better than sitting around waiting for people to phone with news. We were taking control again and it felt good.

The cups of tea kept coming as we remembered more and more. The memories were not as painful now as they had been when I was dredging them up for the book, because now we were working towards a definite goal. Our guardian angels had finally arrived and we were breathless with the excitement of it all. I wanted to give them every bit of information I could think of.

'They're not detailed enough,' I said one evening as we looked at all the drawings we had done. 'They need to know exact distances between the various locations. They need to know exactly how high these mountains are so that they will know what they can see from them and when they will be visible to the villagers. We need to find proper maps of Yemen.'

The next day I tried all the bookshops in Birmingham, but none of them could come up with anything more detailed than an atlas which only showed the major towns. I asked one of the assistants for help and she recommended a travel and map shop in London.

The next day I was on the train to London. The map shop was on Long Acre, between Covent Garden and Leicester Square. They had every imaginable book on every imaginable destination in the world. I wished that we had known about this place before. Mum wouldn't have had so much difficulty pinpointing us once we had made contact if she had had maps like these. I bought one which even named the villages of Ashube and Hockail, and headed back home to Birmingham.

My heart was pounding with excitement. This time we were going to do it. We were going to get them back, even if we had to employ violent men to achieve it. Now I wanted to meet the men myself who were going to carry out the mission.

'I'll set up another meeting,' Mum promised.

A few days later we were told to be at a Post House hotel on the outskirts of Birmingham. As we parked outside the bleak, business-like hotel I felt the butterflies fluttering in my stomach. I could see that Mum was tense, staring straight ahead of her and saying nothing, lost in her own thoughts. We climbed out of the car and went into the hotel.

Two men and two women were waiting for us in the lobby area. One of the women was Judy. She recognised Mum as we approached and they all stood up to greet us. The other woman, who told us her name was Jackie, had an English accent. Judy and the two men – her husband, Don Feeney, and Ken, a big, quiet bloke, who was introduced as a long-time buddy of Don's – were Americans.

Don seemed to be the boss. He apologised to Mum for not having met her before, but he had been caught trying to smuggle some children out of Iceland and been put in prison. That was why Judy had held the preliminary meeting. Don was a very ordinary-looking man, not that tall, with short hair, dressed casually in jeans and a shirt.

I asked about the man whose picture had been on the cover of the book. I think I had imagined it would be him we would be dealing with.

'Dave is no longer involved in active missions,' we were told. 'But he's still very involved with the organisation. We still use his ranch for training exercises.'

They were the most relaxed and comfortable group of people I had ever met. I immediately felt that we were in safe hands. It was as if God had finally answered all the prayers that I had been sobbing into my pillow. He had sent a group of calm, competent, highly trained people who were going to make all our troubles disappear. Everything was going to be all right. All we had to do was give them the information they needed and then wait for them to tell us what would happen next.

When you are as desperate as Mum and I were by that stage, you will do anything and believe anyone who promises you a way out. As we recounted our story once more, both the women started to cry. Their emotion seemed totally genuine. These people made us feel so optimistic about the future!

The men questioned me closely for hours, with the map laid out on the table in front of us. They talked like soldiers, men of action who knew how to take charge of dangerous situations. They told us how the Yemenis had lowered their radar during the Iran–Iraq war, which would make it difficult to fly in and out.

'We will have to stay very low to the ground,' they said. I could do nothing but nod as if I understood what they were talking about. I was happy to leave it up to them. James Bond had become real to me.

'We don't see any problems here,' they said eventually. 'This should be a quick "in and out". It will be an inside job, mainly on the ground. Because there are so many children involved, we will need to take in eight to ten men, all equipped with camouflage uniforms and stun guns.'

'You'll need them,' I said. 'You've got no idea how protective these people are about the British kids they've managed to get their hands on. If they catch you they will shoot you. You may also need to use something to pacify Nadia herself because she will probably be petrified and won't know what is going on. She will be looking to protect the kids.'

'The kids won't be a problem,' they assured us. 'That is why we are going in with such a big team.'

'After your first meeting with Judy,' Don said to Mum, 'we sent a couple of our men into Yemen to take a look around. They took some pictures.'

He spread the enlarged prints out on the table in front of us. I gave a gasp of astonishment. They had actually penetrated all the way to Ashube and photographed Nadia's roof from the mountainside above. They had reached a village which we had frequently been told by diplomats was 'impossible to get to'. They had actually been there and returned with reconnaissance pictures. I could hardly believe what I was looking at. The pictures were so sharp and detailed it was almost like being there and seeing it with my own eyes again. I felt tears welling up as I imagined that Nadia would actually have been inside the house as they were photographing it. They were that close to her.

It seemed that they were halfway towards getting her out already. Another picture showed one of the rescuers posing by a sign to Mokbana. A shiver went right through me as I remembered going past that sign the first time I was driven out to the village.

'We will lift them out by helicopter,' Don explained. 'We have found the best position for the chopper to be waiting, so we can get to it quickly and be away before the men know what has hit them. And we need to have a ship ready to fly everyone out to.'

'Where will the ship be waiting?' I wanted to know.

He spread the map out again and pointed to the southern-most point of the Red Sea, where Yemen almost reached across to Africa.

'There,' he said, 'in Djibouti. It's a French-speaking port, the major one for the Gulf of Aden. It's Ethiopia's main outlet to the sea.'

'Good,' I said, 'if it's French that's all the better. The French government have done more to try to help us than anyone else.'

'We want to go in during Ramadan,' Don said, 'when every-one is fasting and sleeping during the day. That way they will be less alert and there will be fewer men out and about. By the time they've woken up to what is going on we will already be in the air.'

They seemed so efficient and in control I couldn't believe that no one had been able to talk like this to us before. The consulate people had never shown half the initiative that these people had, and it was supposed to be part of their job.

They had made a few token attempts over the years to check that Nadia was all right, but I knew for a fact that when one woman from the consulate went to interview Nadia after the

French publicity, she talked to the wrong woman. She wasn't even in the right house. She went to a much smarter part of the Mokbana region and interviewed a heavily veiled girl who could hardly speak English.

In her report the woman talked about the 'lovely scenery' which Nadia had to look at and a house full of 'mod cons'. She quoted Nadia as saying things like, 'me no want to go home'.

Anyone who has actually spoken to Nadia knows that when she speaks English she still sounds like a native Brummie. Reports like this, which were so obviously inaccurate, had entered the archives with the official stamp of approval. They had become accepted as truth. Every time we went back to argue our case afresh, we had to explain why it was impossible that Nadia would ever have had such a conversation, which meant that we had to call a British official a liar, or at least suggest that he or she was incompetent.

Over the years we had received several of these 'official' reports on Nadia's condition. They always arrived out of the blue. Usually we didn't even know that anyone was going in to see her. In one, the official said that Nadia was fine and healthy, 'although in my personal opinion she seemed dazed and drugged'.

A letter like this would arrive unexpectedly and we would be left with horrific pictures in our minds of the state Nadia must be in, with no way of getting help to her, or of finding out the true situation.

I felt we could now put all the bureaucratic bungling behind us. By the time we had finished that meeting in the hotel, I was willing to put all our lives into these people's hands. Reluctantly, they said that we were now going to have to talk about the money. At that moment, I would have given them anything I could have laid my hands on. The royalties from the book had started to build up. In my mind I had always seen any money that I managed to raise as being part of a fighting fund for getting Nadia and the kids home. If these people could achieve it I would happily hand over everything I had earned so far, plus anything the book would earn in the future.

The timing seemed good. I had just received a cheque for around £100,000 from the French publishers. As far as I was concerned it was unreal money, out of proportion to anything else in my life. I could hardly believe the number of noughts on the cheque which the literary agent had forwarded to me. It would make no difference to me what happened to the money as long as I had Nadia back with me in England. Don told us that they would begin setting up the operation immediately and would keep us posted on their progress. We were going to have to be patient – something that we were experienced at.

In my more optimistic moments, I believed that these Americans were going to prove to be our saviours. I imagined them making their plans and organising their little private army, buying guns and hiring a helicopter and a ship. I allowed myself to believe that we were finally approaching the climax of our story and the end of Nadia's ordeal.

Mum would tell me whenever they needed more money. I was happy to pay it. I knew that an operation like this was bound to be expensive. First they asked for £20,000 to cover their setting up costs. Arrangements were made for the money to travel straight from my bank account to the account of a company in the United States known as CTU. Apparently the company had been set up specially to handle this job. I didn't care what arrangements they wanted to make for their administration. The air of mystery which surrounded the business side of it seemed in keeping with the whole operation. We were, after all, operating outside the boundaries of international law. We had to expect that our new allies would want to take certain precautions.

They asked for another meeting and we arranged it at the house of a friend of Mum's. By that time they had done a lot more research and we were impressed by their findings and the detail of their plans. We seemed to be drawing close to the day when they would be ready to swoop into Mokbana. By the time we had finished talking it was mid-afternoon. They told us that they needed another cheque to go on to the next stage. They were in a rush because they were flying out that night.

'The banks will be closing in a minute,' I said. 'I'll have to phone them and tell them that we are coming in for the money.'

Mum and I then drove like hell into the centre of town, knowing that the bank was in the process of closing up for the day. We made it just in time. We drew out the money, rushed back with it and handed it over.

Within a few months they had had £85,000 from us and said they were ready to go in and carry out the mission. My sense of optimism grew, along with anxiety that if anything went wrong Nadia and the children might end up actually being hurt. I forced these doubts to the back of my mind. It was a risk we had to take. The Americans had assured us that they had covered every eventuality. We had to put our faith in them. They were easy people to trust.

Mum was in touch with them almost every day. She had mobile phone numbers and would never know where they were going to be when she called. Sometimes she would talk to them two or three times a day to reassure herself that they were still there for her. She received a £500 phone bill which I gladly paid off for her.

She and Jana even flew over to Carolina to visit the team and take them more money. They went to their homes and met their families. Mum felt confident that they were doing everything they could to get the operation under way.

They kept telling us they were doing other jobs at the same time as setting up ours, which explained why they were always travelling when we tried to contact them. We would have liked to think that they were dedicating themselves to our case, but in a way it was encouraging to know that their services were so in demand and they were gaining experience on rescues all over the world.

Their confidence that they would be able to get Nadia and the children out never faltered, and we allowed them to convince us of how good the odds were. Mum did notice that they never seemed to ring her. It was always the other way round, but she assumed that was because they were such busy people.

They were very honest about telling us that not all their jobs went as smoothly as they would have liked. They pointed out that there was always an element of risk involved, which we completely understood. They were, after all, breaking the law and might end up being arrested as Don had been in Iceland. They always had highly believable explanations for any delays.

It seemed we were back to waiting again, but at least this time we knew that something was being done and we had someone we could talk to about progress. It was not as if we were waiting for Mohammed or Gowad to fulfil a promise they had made in the heat of some argument, or for an MP who had promised to 'investigate and get back to us'.

A year after our first meeting the Americans rang to say they were now ready to go in and needed another £100,000 to put everything into motion. The fact that they had taken so long to get to this stage made us think that they must have been doing some very thorough groundwork and preparation.

If they had asked for such a huge amount of money right at the beginning we probably would have been less willing to pay. I knew from other sources that they normally didn't charge more than £80,000 in total for a rescue operation and I was surprised that the price for ours was going up so high. But I trusted them completely. It seemed that they had done everything they had promised so far.

'Why is it costing so much?' I asked Mum.

'It's because of all the kids,' she explained. 'They've never done a mission with so many kids involved before. It needs more men and more organisation. They can't take as many risks.'

The explanation seemed reasonable. I was willing to let

them have the money in order to go ahead. I thought Mum and Jana must know what they were doing. After all, they had been dealing with the Americans regularly for a long time by then. The money was paid into their bank account, making the grand total £185,000, and we waited to hear that the mission was under way or completed.

As the days turned into weeks I tried not to think about what might be happening. I just prayed that they were going to surprise us one day soon, and got on with living my daily life. Sometimes I would ask Mum if she had had any news and why it had all gone so quiet. There was always a really good excuse; some other job had come up, or it wasn't the right time of year, or there were problems with their people.

They always seemed to know what was going on in Yemen and that provided them with plenty of reasons not to act. If a VIP was staying in Taiz and security had been increased, for example, it would be a bad time to go in. They were the professionals and we trusted their judgement. The fact that they kept such a close watch on events in Yemen made us feel that at least they were close to acting.

Mum was always convinced by everything they told her and so I was willing to go along with it. I didn't want them to go charging into Mokbana unless they were sure it was the best possible moment. I knew there would only be one chance with a mission like this and if they blew it they would never get another.

So I kept quiet, bottling up my growing disquiet inside me. I didn't have the energy to take an active part in the communications about the operation, I was happy to leave it all to

Mum, knowing that she would keep in touch with me if there were any major developments.

The weeks, however, turned into months and still we heard nothing. If I was feeling optimistic I would imagine that the operation was under way and I would feel a surge of excitement at the thought that Nadia was finally on her way home. At low moments, I would decide that it was never going to happen, or that they had set out and met with some catastrophe along the way.

Eventually, I noticed that Mum was starting to become agitated. She was distracted and irritable when we talked, and she chain-smoked all the time. I could tell that there was something going on in her mind that she wasn't telling me about.

'Something's bothering you,' I said when we were together one day. 'What's going on?'

To begin with she wouldn't say. She was evasive and she tried to change the subject, but I didn't give up. We sat down and went on talking until eventually she started to admit that she was beginning to have her doubts about whether anything was ever going to happen with the Americans.

'They're not doing anything,' she said, her voice tight with pent-up emotion.

'Don't rush them, Mum,' I said, trying to calm her down, despite the fact that I sometimes suffered the same doubts myself. I couldn't bear the thought of her losing the little bit of hope which she had been hanging on to since the Americans had come on the scene.

'If they are going to do something they will do it in their own time. They might just surprise us one day. We'll receive a phone call and be whisked off to go and meet her somewhere. There have been so many years of waiting and suffering, we don't mind hanging on a little bit longer, do we?'

But then it became harder to contact them by phone. The mobile numbers could no longer be reached. Mum would call their homes in Carolina and their kids would answer. 'No, Dad's not here,' they would say. 'He's in another country. We don't have another number.'

More and more I was starting to think that we had been ripped off and that we were never going to see them or the money again. Once more we were waiting in a void, with no idea what was going to happen next. What actually happened was something I had never anticipated.

7

The Accountant and the
Tax Inspector

At first, whenever I received a letter or a bill from any government tax office I would pay whatever I was asked for. There was plenty of money coming in and I had no idea what I was supposed to be paying, so I waited to be told. I had never handled money before. I was fifteen when I first left England and certainly never had any money while I was in Yemen – the men handled all the financial matters in the villages.

The few jobs which I had done when I first got back to England, like working in a factory, had been for bosses who had taken care of any taxes that might be incurred. I had just taken whatever they gave me at the end of the week and asked no questions. Money was never of any interest to me.

If I received a letter asking, for instance, for a national insurance payment I would go round to the tax office in the city centre and give them a cheque. They would give me a

145

receipt and I would go home feeling that I had sorted everything out. I had no idea that I was supposed to be doing anything further.

When the big royalty payments started coming through from countries like France and Germany I would put them into my bank account and draw money out whenever I needed it for something. They seemed to be such enormous amounts that I couldn't imagine that we would ever be able to spend it all. If the tax office had asked for their share I would happily have given it to them. I did not realise that there was a year's grace before the tax bills started to come in and that I was legally obliged to take responsibility for meeting them. Even if I had known, I probably wouldn't have acted any differently. There seemed to be enough money to do everything. But I hadn't reckoned on CTU talking us into transferring nearly £200,000 into their account.

By the time I began to get tax bills for tens of thousands of pounds, I didn't have any money to pay them. The bulk of it had been paid to CTU in America and the rest had vanished into keeping up the campaign for Nadia's release, or helping out friends and relatives whenever they were in trouble. I had just been writing cheques and drawing out cash whenever I felt like it, with no idea how much might be left each time. There had been the phone bills, and the trip to Yemen for Mum and Jana. It had all added up and now there was nothing left in the bank.

I had no idea what to do, so I decided to do nothing in the stupid hope that the problem would just go away. Perhaps, I told myself, my literary agent would send through another big cheque and then I would be able to go round to the tax office and sort things out. I decided to wait and see what happened. I ignored the letters and bills. They began to build into a pile in the corner of the room and I blocked them out of my mind, waiting for something to turn up. It was one thing too many for me to have to think about. Eventually, however, I mentioned the problem in passing to Mum and Jana.

'You should get an accountant,' Jana told me. 'This won't just go away, Zana. They will keep after you until you pay.'

'What's an accountant?' I asked.

'Someone who understands all this stuff,' she waved the forms in the air, 'who will tell you what you owe and what you should pay.'

'I don't know any accountants.' I protested. 'I don't know anything about any of it.'

'I can give you a name,' she said. 'I'll contact him for you if you like.'

By then Jana had proved herself to be a true friend to Mum and me many times over, and we both knew that she was much more worldly than we were. We trusted her to guide us in matters like this. True to her word she put me in touch with Michael in London. A couple of weeks later we went down to meet him, taking with us a bag full of the tax man's letters and other bits of paper.

I was very nervous. Now that I had talked the situation over with Jana I realised that I had got myself into a terrible mess. No more big cheques had arrived and my literary agent told me that I had had all the money that was owing for the moment. There would be other payments coming, but not enough to cover bills this size. As far as the tax people were concerned it was going to look as if I had deliberately defrauded them. I had earned a fortune and within a couple of years it had vanished, with virtually no tax paid at all. I began to get visions of being sent to prison and of being in debt for the rest of my life.

Michael was very friendly. He sat me down in his office and listened to the whole story. I expect he could see what a state I had got myself into because he put no pressure on me at all. I explained about the book and how it had made so much money and I told him how it had all disappeared and how much I had given to the Americans. I could see that he was astounded. I don't suppose he had ever met someone who had managed to get themselves in quite such a huge mess so quickly. I dare say he thought I was incredibly gullible and a fool, but if he did he was much too kind to say anything. I suppose if there weren't a lot of people like me around, accountants like him wouldn't have a job.

He kept asking me questions, the same questions that I guess he knew the tax inspectors were going to be asking him when he tried to explain to them what had happened. I felt terrible. Even though he was being as gentle as he could be, it was as if I was in the witness box in court, being accused of stealing the money.

I felt like a criminal as I tried to answer each question honestly, smoking all the time to cover my nerves. Sometimes I had trouble simply remembering everything that had happened. I gave him the pile of papers which I had been building up at the flat and all the details of the payments we had made to CTU, which my bank had managed to produce for me.

'You go back home,' he said, 'and leave it with me. I will have to work out the best way to approach the problem. Don't panic. We will sort it out.'

I could see that he was having trouble taking it all in and was going to need a little time to reflect on everything I had told him and study all the papers. He seemed a very decent man and Jana said that he had helped her a lot with her problems, so I was more than happy to put my fate in his hands. Just as I trusted him, I could tell that he believed I was not trying to con him. I had been naïve and stupid to spend the money without thinking about paying the tax first, but I hadn't deliberately defrauded anyone. There were no secret bank accounts on offshore islands. Nor was I living in a big detached house or driving around in a brand new Mercedes. I had simply lived for the moment, spending money on things I wanted, helping people who asked to be helped and then I'd given the rest to the Americans. There were no grey areas. There was no mystery about where the money had gone.

I had listened to everything Michael told me as if I was in a daze. The information didn't go in at first, but once we were out of the office I began to think it over. By the time I got back to Birmingham I felt so tense and wound up I didn't know how I was going to cope. I could see now that I was in big trouble. On top of all our other problems I had managed to get into debt to the Inland Revenue. All the money which we had managed to make had vanished and I was sure that, whatever Michael said, I was going to be accused of defrauding the tax people.

In my depression I could imagine myself ending up in

prison, and what would happen to Liam and Cyan then? There had been so much money coming in and I hadn't even taken the time to take them on a holiday to CenterParcs or anything, and now it was too late. There was nothing left for them, or for Nadia if she ever came back. I could feel the weight of the world pressing down on me. I didn't think I was going to be able to hold myself together for much longer.

Jana saw what a state I was in and rang Michael a few days later. 'She's not going to be able to cope,' she told him. 'She's on the verge of a nervous breakdown. You're going to have to leave it for a while.'

He was very understanding and told Jana that he would start talking to the tax people on my behalf and that I wouldn't need to be involved just yet.

As far as I was concerned everything went quiet for a few weeks. I tried to get on with my life, pretending that none of it was happening, looking after Liam and Cyan and going to see friends and relatives. Occasionally I would remember what must be going on behind the scenes and would feel an overwhelming desire to give up the fight. But gradually my strength and confidence began to return. By the time Michael contacted me and asked if I could go back to his office to meet someone from the tax office, I felt able to face it.

If I was tense going to meet Michael the first time, this was a hundred times worse and I was shaking with nerves by the time I got to the office. I imagined that this tax inspector was going to be an ogre, like the sort of stone-faced robots who administer driving tests, never talking to you or meeting your eye, just barking orders.

As the train carrying Jana, Mum and me rumbled towards London, I imagined the inquisition scene which was awaiting me. I was going to feel like a criminal again, as if I had deliberately taken the money and hidden it in a Swiss bank. I was becoming convinced that I was going to end up in jail. I was chain-smoking, my hands trembling as I lit each new cigarette.

Mr Smart was not at all what I imagined a tax inspector would be. He was as friendly and as concerned about me as Michael had been. He had travelled all the way down from Scotland to meet me and now I know that he had some connection to the Fraud Squad. Michael, however, had thought it better not to share that piece of information with me at the time in case it did my head in completely.

The fact that we had the CTU team's names, addresses and bank account numbers made a huge difference to his attitude. I had brought them all with me. Mr Smart was delighted and seemed quite surprised.

'This is excellent,' he said happily. 'I had been afraid that you would come here today and tell me that you had given the money to them and had no paperwork. That would have made my job very hard. With this information we can look them up on our computers. Then at least we'll have something to hand over to the IRS, which is the American equivalent of the Inland Revenue. They will then try to get at least some of the money back.'

He took away the file of papers and we returned home. I felt much better, even though I was aware that I still had a huge tax debt hanging over me. I might not be in danger of being prosecuted or put into prison, but I was still as broke as it is

151

possible to be. Mr Smart went back to Scotland to start working on the computer files and we went back to waiting, having no idea what was going on behind the scenes.

While the tax authorities were digging around in America, Michael was setting about the task of trying to straighten out my accounts to try to work out exactly what I did owe them. He kept asking me for receipts for everything I had spent in the years that the book had been earning advances and royalties, and for the paperwork from my literary agent. He needed to prove how much money had actually come in and to explain where it had all gone.

Day by day, as Michael patiently explained things to me down the phone, I was starting to understand how the system worked. I could now see where I had gone wrong. I understood that by writing the book I had set myself up as a self-employed person, and that there were rules and regulations covering that which I had not bothered to find out about and no one had fully explained to me. Step by step I was getting there.

Not realising that the tax authorities were creeping up on them, the Americans still kept in sporadic contact with Mum. Perhaps they hoped that they would be able to come back for more money. Every so often Mum would receive a phone call from them, assuring her that they were still involved and hadn't forgotten her. They still had a fund of good explanations for their lack of results, usually that other cases had been coming up which were more urgent and which they had known would have fast solutions. Our assignment was more complex, they said, and they needed to be sure that everything was perfect before they moved.

Although there were moments when I liked to believe that they were telling the truth and were just waiting for the right moment to pounce, most of the time I knew that the money had gone and there was nothing I could do about it. Mum didn't argue with them or accuse them of cheating us. She too wanted to believe that there might still be a chance they were genuine. She was also frightened of them. These were people who had managed to convince us that they would use guns to achieve their goals. Mum didn't want to make enemies of them.

Sold was still selling steadily all over Europe and almost every month one or other of the publishers would ring and ask me to go to their country to do another round of interviews. I would nearly always go, but it was becoming harder and harder to do. I had no spare reserves of energy left. It was as if I was working on automatic pilot, trying to cope with Liam and Cyan, trying to answer Michael's questions, worrying about Mum, trying to take in the constant travel arrangements that were being made for me; getting to and from airports, picking up tickets, getting to hotels, going through the whole story again for another journalist who knew nothing about it. My head was spinning.

I didn't want to let any of the publishers down because they had been so supportive and helpful in getting our story heard around the world. The French in particular had been amazing. They had sold over a million copies of the book by then and done everything they could to help us. The fact that they hadn't succeeded in getting Nadia out was certainly not due to lack of commitment or effort on their part.

In the early days I had been so full of energy. I had been able to do interviews for hours on end, answering the same questions over and over again. I had been so sure that if I kept up the pressure we would have Nadia free in no time. When the months turned into years, I found my energy draining away and I began to become less obliging to people who I thought were asking stupid questions or didn't seem to be completely on our side. I was so tired that sometimes I was less than pleasant to the journalists and television crews who were wheeled in to talk to me, firing questions at me from every angle.

'Listen,' I snapped on one occasion when they kept interrupting me and I felt as if I had been awake for ever, 'you need me to get your stories. I don't need you. So you chill out and let me say what I want to say. You listen and you write or do whatever you have to do, and then go.'

At moments like this it all began to seem futile. What was the point of going on and on trying to get publicity for the case if the Yemenis didn't care? Had it all been a huge waste of time? I wondered. Then I would manage to get a little rest, or someone would say something encouraging and I would find the willpower to get going again. I couldn't think of anything else to do and I couldn't possibly sit around doing nothing, knowing that Nadia was still out there, waiting for me to keep my promise.

When the IRS went in search of CTU in America, they found that the company we had paid all the money to had ceased trading. It had been set up just to deal with our payments. Now our money had been moved out and the company closed down. The trail seemed to go dead. Further investigations revealed that the same people had set up a number of other companies, one for each assignment presumably, which had also vanished into thin air. One of them was called 'The No Longer Trading Company', which seemed pretty cheeky, sticking a finger up to anyone who was trying to track them down.

Mr Smart called us to a meeting and told us that when the IRS went to freeze the deeds on the properties owned by the people we had met, they found that they actually owned nothing. All their homes and offices seemed to be rented, so that they could pack up and move on as soon as things started to go wrong. They appeared to be classic con-men and women. We could only pray that all the evidence that was building up was wrong, and that they just had to stay mobile for security reasons. It was becoming increasingly hard to keep any faith at all.

Meanwhile, Mum and I were constantly trying to think of new ways to draw the world's attention to Nadia's plight. Although we had lost all the money which *Sold* had earned for us, and although reliving the experience over and over again on the publicity tours had been agonising, publishing a book had been by far the most effective thing we had done to raise awareness of our story.

When Mum told me that she was thinking about writing a book herself about her life and experiences, I had mixed feelings. I was worried that she would find it a terrible ordeal, not only to write it but to go out on the road to promote it. I knew how hard I had found it, and Mum's health was a great deal more delicate than mine. At the same time I had to admit it would be a brilliant way to bring our story back to public attention.

Although *Sold* was still on bookshelves all over the world, and although it had been turned into a successful radio play, it was no longer newsworthy. I was asked to do fewer and fewer interviews. In one way that was a relief – it allowed me to get on with the job of bringing up my children – but at the same time I was desperate to keep up the pressure on the British and Yemeni governments to do something. Another book would mean another round of interviews and reviews. Maybe this time we would be lucky and reach the right people. Mum might also be able to earn a bit of money so that she could go out to Yemen again if an opportunity arose; or we could afford to pay for tickets for Nadia and the children – or whatever else Mohammed might ask of us. On balance, another book had to be a good idea.

I knew that Mum wouldn't be capable of writing it on her own. The strain would have been far too much for her. Her brain was so full of facts and dates and arguments, she would never have been able to sort them out into a simple enough form for readers to make head or tail of them. There had been so many hundreds of conversations with diplomats and politicians, journalists and publishers. There were mountains of letters and forms and court papers to be sorted through. The effort would have killed her. She had to find someone to work with her.

She decided to write the book with Jana, which I thought was a good idea. To start with, she trusted Jana completely, plus they had been through an amazing amount together. Opening herself up to Jana would not be a problem, and Jana already knew as much, if not more, of the details of the story anyway.

Jana has the most incredible memory, which makes her very useful to Mum. Mum is so distracted by the pressures of day to day existence that she often forgets critical events or dates. Jana never forgets anything. If Mum is telling a story and can't remember a name or a sequence of events, Jana can always fill it in.

On top of that she has great computer skills, which Mum most definitely hasn't, so she could easily do the actual writing of the manuscript, making Mum's words flow and make sense to the readers.

The idea was that the book would cover Mum's life from when she left home as a teenager up to the present day. It would show how she had met Dad and how he came to dominate her in the traditional Muslim way. It would talk about how he took their first two children, Laila and Ahmed, off to Yemen so that she didn't see them again until they were grown-ups. It would then give her side of the story about how Nadia and I had disappeared. During the eight years that we were both in Mokbana, her life had been a living nightmare as she frantically tried to find us and get us out, feeling that she ran into brick walls wherever she turned.

It had been a great turning point in Mum's life. Until then she had been a typically submissive woman, allowing Dad to walk all over her. She had had seven children by him and been treated like dirt. She had suffered two nervous breakdowns as a result of the stresses he had inflicted on her.

The thought of losing Nadia and me in the same way as Laila and Ahmed was too much. It forced her to turn round and fight back for the first time. She was also determined to save Tina, Ashia and Mo from the same fate. She parted from Dad and started on her long crusade, raising support for our cause and going to the media and the government. The pressure ruined what was left of her health but she still refused to give up the fight. The book was called *Without Mercy*. It was subtitled 'A Mother's Struggle Against Modern Slavery'.

The story went on to tell of all her attempts after I returned to get Nadia and the children out. The book helped to explain to people who were familiar with our story, some of the background as to how she came to be fooled by Dad, and would answer some of the questions which people kept writing to me about after reading *Sold*.

She told my agent about the idea and he sold it to the same British publishers as *Sold*. Mum then started to disappear for whole days into Jana's house, coming home late at night with pages and pages of computer print-out. I don't know if Mum would have been able to get through the whole experience if she hadn't had Jana's help. They were an amazing team. I couldn't bring myself to read any of it – I have never been able to read *Sold* either, or listen to the radio adaptation which the BBC did. I knew it would be too harrowing for me. I was aware of all the facts, I didn't need to torture myself with them all over again.

The manuscript they produced in the end weighed three kilograms and the publishers had to cut over half the material out in order to bring it to a publishable length. There was just too much to be said and they didn't think that readers would be able to cope with it.

Without Mercy was published in 1995, laying out all the horrors of Mum's life. It received some very good reviews in the British press. We were back on the bookstalls and back in the pages of the newspapers. Perhaps this time we would find the right person to champion our cause.

8

'This is a Great Story'

The money from the book had come in so easily, I suppose I had imagined that it would keep on coming and that it was a bottomless pit. But I knew now, from talking to Michael and to my agent, that the flow of cash was slowing down dramatically. I now understood that most best-sellers only stay at the top of the charts for a few months, maybe a year if they are lucky. Once everyone who is interested has bought the book, sales drop dramatically and, a few months later, the income drops accordingly.

Michael had been working hard at sorting out every detail of my affairs over the previous few years and he had reached an agreement with Mr Smart who realised that I had no way of paying the full amount. He was willing to settle for a very reduced payment, much less than they had originally asked for, in the hope that he would be able to get the balance back from the Americans. From then on, whenever any royalty cheques came in, my agent would send them straight to the tax office. Once I had paid off the debt owing, then the money would start coming back to me. Even though the amount owing had been reduced, it didn't look as if the amounts coming in would ever cover it. It was like throwing pebbles into a bottomless well.

Mr Smart had said that if the Inland Revenue managed to get any money back from the Americans they would take what they were owed and give me back the rest. It seemed like a fair deal to me, but very depressing. All we could do was hang on and hope that it would happen. We were back, once again, to waiting.

Now the money had gone we had to keep searching for other ways to help Nadia. We have had to adjust our living standards dramatically. I'm now on income support and child benefit, and Paul has his disability allowance, but together that only gives us about £160 a week on which to live. We can just about manage, though there is virtually nothing in the kitty by the weekend. We are careful to find the best bargains in the supermarkets, and I have become an expert on the charity shops around Mum's house. I buy most of the children's clothes from the cancer shop, and I get books from the Age Concern shop. When Mark had an accident while we were out and I needed to change him urgently, I managed to get him a complete outfit of sweatshirt and jeans for £1.50. I even buy some of my Christmas presents from charity shops. It doesn't bother me. As long as we have enough to feed and clothe ourselves and the kids, I'm content. I know that once I have finished my training as a swimming instructor I will be able to earn again, and hope-fully get another car to help with getting the kids to school.

I didn't feel too bad about losing the money to the mercenaries until I saw the Englishwoman, Jackie, appearing on a breakfast television show. She had written a book about her adventures, including details of our case, and the cameras showed the luxurious house and car which she had bought with the proceeds of her activities. I felt that I was watching money which should have been spent on my children being flaunted in my face by someone else.

When Mum first showed me a letter which she had received from another documentary-maker called Nick Gray, I told her I didn't want to know. We had already had dealings with one film-maker interested in our story, which had come to nothing, leaving us with our fingers burned. I felt that we were sitting ducks for anyone who held out the slightest hope that we might be able to get Nadia freed. I couldn't face the thought of getting my hopes up again, just to have them dashed once more. 'Don't talk to me about anybody,' I told her. 'Leave me alone. Let me just get on with my life. The money's all gone, we are going to have to find another route to saving Nadia. We'll start up the campaign again, go on marches, whatever, but no more television documentaries.'

Mum started laughing but I could tell it was a nervous laugh. She knew that I had been pushed to my limit, because she felt the same, but she couldn't resist grabbing at every straw which floated past. She must have dreaded the thought of being let down again as much as I did, but she couldn't bring herself to let an opportunity pass, however slim it might seem. She took no notice of my ill temper and set about talking me round. It didn't take long before I grudgingly agreed to meet the man with her.

I went to the meeting with a face like thunder, preparing myself to see through Mr Gray in a moment. I was ready to mock any promises which he might make to us. If he was willing to go ahead despite my unpleasantness, I reasoned, then he might just stand a chance. It would be like a sort of test. If he gave up too easily he would not have been any use to us anyway. We needed someone who would be able to put up with any amount of obstruction and aggravation from everyone that he came across in the process of the investigation.

He seemed very genuine. He listened to our story, although we decided not to say anything about the Americans at this stage. Now that we were beginning to believe that they had deliberately defrauded us, they had started to seem rather dangerous and sinister in our minds. As long as we had thought they were on our side we had felt comfortable with their military ways and their talk of violent action. Now it was as if they had become our enemies, and that made us very nervous.

'These people are capable of anything,' I told Mum one day when we were discussing them. 'They could just turn up in your back garden and shoot you dead. We know they're capable of it because of the things they've done in the past. We can't afford to upset them.'

Nick was very patient at that first meeting. Perhaps he had talked to other people who had warned him that I could be difficult sometimes. He seemed to understand that I was under stress. He didn't appear to be taking any of it personally. I used words I didn't even know I knew at one stage in the discussion.

I was just so tired of people coming along and getting our hopes up. He kept very quiet, listening to everything I had to say and not trying to protest or argue, a bit like a therapist. I think I deliberately tried to shock him out of his quiet acceptance of everything I was telling him. I didn't care what sort of bad impression I made on anyone by this time. I was even being nasty to my own family for a while. Once I had ground to a halt, unable to think of anything else to say in the face of his boundless patience, he said he would like to do a programme.

'I'll leave it with you,' he said as he got up to go. 'If you decide to go ahead with it then contact me and we'll make the film.'

Once he had gone I still felt the same as when Mum first mentioned his letter. I just couldn't bring myself to start on the long haul of emotional turmoil that I knew a documentary would involve. I didn't want to have to go through hours of new interviews, reliving all the horrors yet again. I didn't want to have to listen to tapes of Nadia or see pictures of her, knowing that she was still waiting for me to fulfil my promise to her. The thought of going through all that again, only to be let down once more at the end in some way, was more than I could bear.

Mum must have realised that I needed time to think about it. I started by trying to put it out of my mind, but the idea kept coming back to me. I racked my brains to think of some alternative I could offer to Mum, but I couldn't come up with anything, and in my conscience I kept hearing a little voice telling me that I was passing up an opportunity for Nadia.

Days passed and I was lying in my bed one night, my thoughts going over and over the same territory. 'Haven't I been through enough? I shouldn't be torturing myself in this way,' I thought. 'Everything needs to come out into the open. If we don't keep Nadia's story alive in people's minds then other mothers will lose their children in the same way. Even if this film fails to get Nadia back it might save just one more little girl from suffering the same fate. It might alert some woman to the dangers and stop her from allowing her child to travel to a foreign country without her.' Similarly, if we didn't expose the Americans they could continue ripping off other distressed mothers. I was being offered a chance to do all these things. I had to take it.

When I told Mum of my decision I could see how relieved she was. But she wanted us only to talk about Nadia and the authorities. She said she was too scared of the Americans to risk talking about them yet.

We called Nick Gray the next day and told him that we had decided to go ahead with the project. He invited us to Yorkshire Television in Leeds to meet the producers who were interested in the story and to talk about it.

If we wanted to go ahead we had to sign a contract. I didn't want to sign anything. I was in enough trouble without committing to anything else. Nick was gentle but firm. He told me that he had to have the signature if we were going to go ahead. Eventually I took a deep breath, picked up the pen, closed my eyes and signed. How much worse could things get? This was a chance and I had to keep taking every chance possible. Now that I was committed to the project I could not imagine any alternative.

Nick started to come round to Mum's house with his camera crew and another interviewer called Emma, to film interviews with Mum and me. He made hours and hours of film, so that he had plenty to edit at the end. Emma would start the day by talking to me for three hours or so. At the end of that I would feel drained and would go home for a rest before picking up the children from school or a sitter, while Nick interviewed Mum for a similar length of time.

To begin with we talked about Nadia and about our feelings. I found it very hard to speak to the camera for long without starting to cry. All the barriers which I have put up in my mind against the pain, all the distractions which I have with my daily life, crumble when I actually have to talk about how I feel.

As soon as I do that, I can picture Nadia in that village. I can picture the way in which the men bully and taunt her. I can see the daily struggle which she has to go through. I can feel the ball of hunger which she would have grown so used to feeling in her stomach that she hardly even notices it any more. I can remember the burning heat of the kitchen stove and the grinding toil of preparing the monotonous food. During the day there are the persistent swarms of flies and at night I can imagine her lying on her hard bed, every muscle and joint aching, listening to the distant howling of the wolves in the mountains.

I know how hard it is because I went through it myself. But I was always determined that eventually I would get away and that gave me something to live for, some reason to wake up each morning. I'm sure that most of the time Nadia must have given up all hope of ever escaping. She must believe now that she is doomed to stay locked in that miserable life until the day she dies. She will keep producing children until she is no longer fertile and then she will be an old woman, her life having been drained from her by other people who care nothing for her, who see her as just another piece of livestock, there to work and breed. I can't stop myself from crying when I allow such thoughts to surface, whether there is a camera present or not.

After a few days, when we had become comfortable with Nick, Mum said. 'Shall we tell him about the Americans, Zana?'

By then I felt ready to talk about them and I agreed. I was pleased that Mum had decided she could deal with the subject in the open. I now believed firmly that as long as we kept silent they had got away with it. At least if we came out and challenged them in public they would have to justify themselves in some way. I could see that the American story would also give the film an extra angle. Nick had become like a family friend, and I wanted to trust him with the whole truth. I didn't want what had happened in the past to poison my mind against someone who was genuinely willing to help.

We told them that we had more to tell them. They set the camera running again and we explained everything, from the book being handed across the lunch table in Stockholm to the fruitless phone calls to Carolina and the Philippines and God knows where else.

Once he knew everything, Nick wanted to go out to America and try to get the CTU people on film. 'This is a great story,' he said. 'I could tell them that we are doing a general documentary about saving lost children,' he said. 'They'll jump at the chance of some free publicity. Once I'm there I can mention your case and ask them what happened. They don't have to know that you have worked out they have conned you. We can show both sides of the story and let the viewer decide who they believe. It should be pretty obvious what has happened.

'I also need to take the film crew out to Yemen to get some footage of the places where it all happened, to give people a flavour of the place.'

'You'll never get into the village, or get to Nadia,' I warned.

'I know,' he said. 'But we can still get some background stuff, give the viewer an idea of the atmosphere and the area where you were imprisoned and where Nadia still is. It would be great if you could come with us, so we could film you out there. If you came to Taiz then we might be able to get them to bring Nadia out for a meeting and film it.'

I felt a chill of fear ripple through me at the suggestion. There was no way that I was going back out to Yemen with a film crew. I had heard the rumours that the men had planned to kidnap me when I flew down with the French for the meeting with Nadia in the garden. Mum had also warned me that Abdullah was claiming that he had remarried me. I was terrified that if I went back they would snatch me off the street and no one in England would ever hear of me again.

I was equally certain that Mum shouldn't go down there again either. She could have been murdered during her trip with Jana, and had been attacked by a mob. If she was seen to have come back with a film crew there was no telling how high tempers would run.

Tina and Aisha agreed with me and we all told her that there was no way we would agree to such a plan. Mum, however, was not that easily put off. If there was any chance that she could get to see Nadia again, however much personal danger there might be to herself, she wanted to try. Despite all our advice she contacted the British embassy in Sana'a to ask for an access visa. To my relief, the officials she spoke to were equally adamant that it wouldn't be safe. Mum, however, insisted that she wanted to see her daughter.

'I'll have to send someone to see Nadia first,' the consul said, realising that Mum was not about to be put off easily, 'to ask her if she wants to see you.'

'How dare you?' Mum exploded. 'I'm her mother. I don't need your guys going to ask her if she wants to see me.'

The consul took no notice. He sent someone to see Nadia and her reaction must have been similar to mine when Mum first showed me Nick's letter. She told the emissary that she didn't want any more trouble. It was obvious that she would be given a hard time by Mohammed if Mum persisted in her demands. Our priority had to be getting the film made, not stirring up more trouble. We could see that we would be stumbling straight back into a political minefield if Mum persisted, and the focus of the visit would then be on her rather than on Nadia. We had to think of something better. It was a relief to think Mum would not be going, but we couldn't think who else to send.

'I'll go,' said Mo. We were all surprised. During all the years

170

of waiting for Nadia, our little brother had grown up. He was twenty-four now and he wanted to take his part in the family drama. Now that we thought about it, he was the obvious choice. Because he was a man there was little danger that Dad could arrange for him to be kidnapped, and he had not aggravated anyone in Taiz.

He had been only a young boy when he came with Mum in search of Nadia and me the first time, but at least he knew a little about what to expect. And it would be good for Nadia to see her baby brother again after so long.

Mo had grown into a very confident person. He was working in a factory that made motorised golf caddies for rich people all over the world. Mo used to service and mend them. The caddies would be sent back to the factory for servicing from places as far afield as South America, often with tips enclosed for Mo. The owner of the factory was an Israeli who had read *Sold* and knew all about our story. He was happy to give Mo whatever time off he needed for the trip without docking his pay. Mo always got on with everybody, which was another reason why he was a better person to go to Yemen than Mum or me. He was much less likely to pick fights with people or be unpleasant when things started to go wrong.

Before setting out, Mo decided he should make contact with our father to see if he could find out more details about Nadia's whereabouts and her situation. He needed Dad's help to get in touch with her. I had no problem with that. The bad blood between Dad and me was personal, I didn't expect the others to ostracise him as well.

Many years before, when I was still in Mokbana, Mo had

gone to Dad's place and secretly retrieved a tape and letter which I had sent to Mum but which Dad had intercepted. It had been a brave act for a little boy and it helped to alert Mum to how bad things were for Nadia and me. It had meant, however, that Dad and Mo had not spoken since. Dad had told him he had to choose between him and Mum. Mo chose Mum.

When the idea for Mo's trip came up, it seemed wise that he should go to see Dad to ask whether he would be safe if he travelled to Yemen. We knew that if Dad told everyone down there to leave Mo alone, he would be obeyed. If Dad told Mohammed to bring Nadia into Taiz to meet Mo, then it would happen. Mo needed to let Dad think he wanted to mend bridges between them, so that he could talk to him man-to-man.

He set out for Dad's house without any idea of what sort of reception he might expect. Would Dad agree to see him? Would he rant and rave at him about all the years that Mo had sided with Mum against him? Or would he welcome back his prodigal son with open arms, hoping to recruit him to his side, grasping the opportunity to poison his mind against the women in his family?

9

Mo

It must have taken every ounce of self-control that Mo could muster to be civil to Dad that day, when all he really wanted to do was to hit him.

Because he had been out to Yemen right at the beginning, when Mum came out to try to find us, he knew more about what we had been put through than most people. He had seen the living conditions we had to endure and the way in which we were treated like slaves. Like me he could visualise all too clearly what Nadia was still having to go through every day of her life, while Dad sat around his house in Birmingham and did nothing to save her. One phone call from Dad and Nadia would have been on a plane to England within days.

What he knew made Mo boil with suppressed anger and his instincts were to punch Dad the moment he saw him. But he gritted his teeth as he knocked on the door, knowing that he had to control himself. He had to make Dad believe that he wanted to heal the rift between them. He had to keep telling himself that he was doing it for Nadia and for Mum and that if he messed it up they would suffer.

Dad was still living in Sparkbrook with his new young wife and two kids. When he opened the door and saw Mo standing on the step he must have had mixed feelings, wondering what sort of trouble might be heading his way now. Once he realised that Mo had come to try to be friendly, he was overcome with emotion.

It was similar to the one time I had been back to see him since returning from Yemen. I went round in all my Arab clothes to tell him I loved him and to plead for Nadia to be allowed to come home. He had cried then, and told me how he never realised how badly we had been treated and how he would immediately instruct Mohammed to send Nadia back. None of it meant anything, of course, and I never went to see him again.

Seeing his second son must have made him even more emotional. He ushered Mo into the house and introduced him to his wife and new family.

Dad was always pleased to hear the sound of his own voice and, being nervous in Mo's quiet, serious company, he prattled on about himself. He told Mo that he had been paid £15,000 to marry the girl so that she could get into the country for a big operation that she needed. She had one leg shorter than the other, because of something to do with her hip, and had to wear a built-up shoe as a result. Her family already lived in Birmingham and were friends of his. None of us doubt that the story is true. It sounds like exactly the sort of thing he would do.

What we find puzzling, however, is that when Nadia and I were asking the Foreign Office to get us out of Yemen, they said they couldn't because we were 'dual nationals'. Mum is English, so that must mean that Dad is a Yemeni citizen. If that is so, how can he marry someone in order for them to gain a British passport? He must be British. That means that Nadia and I could never have been dual nationals, we were always British and our government refused to recognise the fact.

Dad and his wife now have four children and I sometimes feel sad that we will never get to know our little half-siblings, but there is no way the two families could be friendly after all that has happened. Our hatred and distrust of Dad is so deep we would never want him to be part of our lives again, and he would never allow us to get close to his new family. I dare say his wife has been brainwashed into believing that we are all prostitutes and profane women who show no respect for our men and should be avoided at all costs. It would be hard to change any ideas that Dad may have planted in her head about us.

A lot of women have been coming to England from the Mokbana region lately. In the old days the men would travel and send back money to their wives and mothers, building up nest eggs for their retirement. But now a change in the tax laws has made it more profitable for them to bring their wives over here too. They can then draw welfare for them and save up the money in England. When they are ready for retirement they take their money back to Yemen with them, where the cost of living is a fraction of what it is in England.

That was what Gowad (Nadia's so-called father-in-law) and his wife, Salama, did. Many years later, when they had saved enough money, they sold their house in Birmingham and returned home to live off the proceeds. I heard from several sources that Gowad died within a few weeks of returning home – which makes me think that there is some justice in life, even if it sometimes comes too late.

No doubt Dad misses Gowad's company. I believe they saw a lot of one another when Gowad was in England, no doubt talking over everything that has happened as they played cards together into the small hours of the morning, plotting and planning how to make life as difficult as possible for the rest of us.

When Gowad and Salama came out of Yemen, leaving Nadia to look after their children, they were supposed to go back within a few months. They had no intention of doing so and Nadia was left with the burden of bringing up their children as well as her own. By the time they returned, the children were grown up. They had another daughter over here and I would sometimes see Gowad taking her to school. She was a big girl, probably as tall as me even though she is only nine or ten years old.

I went to enrol for a dress-making course at a local college in Birmingham a few years ago, and found the classroom full of Yemeni women who couldn't speak a word of English. They were all young and veiled and reminded me of the village girls I had got to know so well when I was out there. I guess most of them would have been brought over to be married to old men like my dad. Probably they would have been sold by their fathers so that they could live in England and send money back to their families: the reverse of what had happened to Nadia and me.

Although living in Birmingham is infinitely more comfortable than living in Mokbana, and hardly any of them ever say that they want to go back once they have grown used to the Western lifestyle – the culture shock when they first arrive in Britain must be just as dramatic as it was for Nadia and me when we arrived in Yemen.

The teacher tried to encourage these girls to unveil for the class, since there were only women in the room, but they wouldn't do it. They must have been feeling very vulnerable and insecure. They were surrounded by their little children – even though they were supposed to use the crèche facilities – just as they would have been in their village homes. I didn't go back to the course. It was taking too long for everything the teacher was saying to be interpreted and there was so much noise from the children that we couldn't get anything done. I had left all that behind me and I didn't want to be reminded of it.

In my mind I would have liked to kill Gowad with my own hands, just as I would like to kill my father and Abdul Khada, the man who took me to Yemen for his son and treated me like a dog for eight years. In reality I know that it would do no good, that it wouldn't help to bring Nadia back. I look the other way when I see any of them on the street in Birmingham, and try not to think of what they did to us.

Although I still blame these three men for creating the situation in the first place, I now feel greater anger towards the government ministers who should have come to our rescue when the people who were supposed to be protecting us let us down. If a parent in England is mistreating his or her child the authorities are quick enough to intervene. Why did we never merit that sort of concern?

Mo went twice to see Dad and both times he came back to us with so much pent-up anger in him that we thought he was going to explode. In the past he had vowed that he would kill Dad if he saw him, and we knew that he meant it. Now Mo had to sit and listen to the old man boasting about his life, and bad-mouthing Mum and me, so that he could get the assistance he needed for the trip.

'Listen,' Mo said to him at the first meeting. 'You're still my dad and I'm still your son. There are family matters which we need to discuss. I want to talk to my sister. I need you to set it up for me. Can you arrange for her to phone you here so that I can talk to her?'

Dad, no doubt pleased to receive such respectful treatment from his son, agreed to get in touch with his agent in Taiz, Nasser Saleh, and organise for Nadia to be brought out of the village to Nasser Saleh's house so she could take a phone call from Mo.

I could remember that house so clearly and Mo told me later that nothing had changed. Whereas many of the people in Taiz had lino on their floors, nice furniture and all the latest electronic equipment, Nasser Saleh was still living down a dirt track in a house with bare concrete floors. He must have been earning enough money from all the people who used him as an agent to buy something better, but he still lived like the most basic of villagers. He was a little weed of a man, always running around doing other people's bidding, but Mo knew that he was going to have to deal with him if he wanted to see Nadia. He also needed to gather evidence for Nick Gray's documentary of how her life was run by the men.

Nasser Saleh then rang back to give Dad a date when Nadia would be there. Mo returned to Dad's house on the appointed day to make the phone call. I was very doubtful about whether they would keep their word and actually have her there.

Nick Gray equipped Mo with a tape and a miniature microphone, so that he could record the conversation and we could all hear what Nadia was saying.

Mo went back to Dad's house, his heart thumping in his chest. If Dad realised he was being set up for a television programme there was no telling how he would react. It would certainly end in a fight and Mo would then not be able to expect any co-operation once he got to Taiz. It was hard enough for Mo to have to think of what to say to Nadia so as not to frighten her, but to be trying to work the tape recorder, and keep it hidden from Dad at the same time, would make everything doubly stressful.

The call went through to Nasser Saleh's house and, miracle of miracles, Nadia was there as promised. It seemed that the men were more willing to co-operate with Mo than they had ever been with us, more willing to keep their word. She came on the line and Mo discreetly set the tape running.

'I'm planning to come over to see you,' he told her after they had been chatting politely for a few moments.

'You what?' Nadia obviously couldn't believe what she was hearing. 'What if I come?'

'What do you mean?' Mo wanted to know.

'What if I come to England with Mohammed and the kids?'

'Are you serious?'

'Yeah,' Nadia said. 'But we need some money for the tickets.'

Mo went silent for a moment as he tried to work out all the angles. Was she speaking for herself, or had she been told to say this? Had they finally come round to the idea of letting her go? Could it really be that easy after so long? Was it a delaying tactic to put him off going to Yemen?

'Well, all right then,' he said, eventually. 'We'll arrange it. I'll come over with the tickets. How many kids are there?'

'Six.'

We'd even lost track of how many children she had.

Once the telephone conversation was over, Mo was keen to get out of the house as quickly as possible to tell us of this dramatic development. He was also desperate to get away from Dad before the microphone was spotted. To leave too soon, however, might have looked suspicious, so he stayed and chatted about his forthcoming trip for a while, before casually getting up and leaving the house and heading back home.

That night he played the tape to Nick and the rest of us. All of us were shocked, hardly able to believe what we were hearing. I was torn between elation at the possibility that she might finally be coming home, and a little voice at the back of my head which was telling me not to get my hopes up because I would only end up having them dashed again.

I knew that Mohammed might well have told Nadia that they could all travel to England. I knew that the British embassy had promised that should the family ever want to travel to England they would ensure that all the paperwork was put through as speedily as was necessary. I just didn't believe that Mohammed would actually have meant it. Once he considered what was likely to happen when he arrived in England, he was sure to go back on any promises he might have made to Nadia. He would have known that once she and the children were safely in Birmingham she would never want to go back to Ashube and he would lose control of her as soon as she had her real family around her again to protect her.

'OK,' Nick said when the tape had finished running. 'We'll get the tickets for you. You'll have to be the one to go down now, Mo. She's expecting you and she seems happy with the idea.'

He must have been thinking just how good an ending it would be for his film if he could actually show Nadia finally coming home after sixteen years. If that happened, I would have been more than happy for him to have filmed it. Every camera in the world could be there for all I cared, as long as Nadia was home.

'You won't be able to film Nadia,' Mo warned Nick. 'If you try to do that you'll mess up everything. You can get your shots of the countryside and of Taiz, and I'll try to get tapes of Nadia talking, but they won't let you near her with cameras. If she finds out there is a camera crew with me, God knows what she'll do.'

I knew he was right. I could remember her reaction to the

French camera crew, and the suspicion she had treated Jana with when she thought she was a journalist. No one in Yemen must know that the film was being made or they would make her life even harder than it already was.

If the programme was ever screened, of course, there would be nothing we could do to stop Mohammed finding out about it, but that was a risk worth taking.

Mo travelled out to Yemen on his own, looking for all the world like a man going on an innocent visit to his sister. We had packed another suitcase full of gifts for her and the children.

Nick and his team followed a few days later, posing as tourists with a video camera.

'Don't worry,' Mo said to me just before he went, 'I'll fetch her home.'

He was so confident and hopeful, I decided to leave him to it. I hoped for all our sakes that he would be able to pull it off. All my first instincts were pessimistic, but I didn't want to drag his spirits down. He had enough worries and pressures without all my usual predictions of gloom and doom. I kept quiet and wished him luck.

Although every part of me wanted to believe that it could happen, I just couldn't see it. I could imagine them bringing Nadia into the city and setting her up in a flat so she could talk to Mo. I could imagine Mohammed and Nasser Saleh allowing Mo a lot of freedom, but watching every move he made.

They would then start putting pressure on Nadia to tell

him that she was happy in Yemen and didn't want to leave. They would want him to come home with a message to Mum and me that it was no good us keeping on fighting because Nadia had made up her mind to stay.

Mo might be able to make her admit the truth to him if he could get her on her own, away from Mohammed, but she would change her tune again immediately if she thought he was recording her words for a television programme.

I didn't like the idea that we weren't able to be open and honest with her about what we were doing, but I knew that she wouldn't be able to understand it and that the idea of more publicity would frighten her. It was a horrible position to be in and I found myself becoming increasingly depressed.

'You're wasting your money with those tickets,' I had told Nick a few days after Mo came back from Dad's house, 'because she won't be coming.'

'I've made an arrangement with the travel agent so that we get a refund if the flights aren't used,' Nick said. 'Just in case.' It didn't sound as if he was much more optimistic than I was. I suppose he had spent so many hours listening to Mum and me talking about the number of times our hopes had been dashed that he couldn't believe that she was finally coming out either.

Once Mo had gone we were all worried about his safety. We knew what had happened to Mum and, although he was a man, we didn't like the idea of the same thing happening to him. After talking to my sisters, Tina and Ashia, I decided that for Mo's sake I would go to see Dad and insist that he allow me to speak to Mo, and with any luck Nadia as well, over the phone while Mo was there. It would make us feel better to be able to talk to them direct and there was no way we could arrange to phone Nadia ourselves.

We knew we could never make contact with Nadia while she was in the village, but in Taiz, while we knew where she was, it was possible. As long as we could persuade Dad to arrange it.

We knew that Mum had made a great many enemies on her visits to Yemen, and we knew that Dad could contact people who would make sure that Mo was looked after and protected. I never believed that Dad would ever wish Mo any harm, but there were others that Mo might need protection from. I wanted to make sure that they all knew Mo was in Taiz with Dad's blessing.

I hadn't actually seen Dad since the time I had confronted him on my return to England in 1988. Ever since then I had deliberately avoided him, afraid that I wouldn't be able to stop myself from flying at him with my fists, or worse, if I looked at him walking freely down the street while Nadia was still a prisoner. I knew that with one word to Gowad or Mohammed he could have ended our whole nightmare, but he didn't have the courage.

He could have told his friends that Nadia was to come back on a visit just as he could have told them to release both of us at any stage during the eight years that I was there too. But he never lifted a finger to help us, even though he was our father and he had caused all our misery. The one time I had seen him he had wept and asked for my forgiveness, but they had been false tears. In the years that had passed since that meeting he had done nothing to change the situation. He had lied to me then as he had lied so many times before.

The thought of walking into his house was almost unbearable. But I knew that if I wanted to keep in touch with Nadia during Mo's stay I would have to go through him. There was no one else. If Mum or I tried to phone Nasser Saleh's house ourselves we would never be put through to Nadia.

I was going to have to go to Dad's house and demand that he arrange the call. That meant that I would have to control my temper and not attack him. Inside my head I would have happily killed him. Outside I had to keep my mouth shut for fear of what I might be unable to stop myself saying, and my eyes lowered for fear that I might look at his smirking face and be unable to control my temper.

Tina, who had kept up contact with him over the years whenever she met him in the street, agreed to come with me. I was going to need someone else to do the talking, not able to trust my own voice under so much emotional strain.

We turned up on his doorstep with no warning. We wanted to take him by surprise, so that he didn't have time to prepare a story about how we were asking the impossible of him, or to go out and leave his young wife to face us alone. He opened the door to our knock and stood staring in horror as I strode past him into the house without a word.

Recovering himself a little, he gave Tina a hug. She responded in a quiet, respectful way. It was impossible to tell from her face what she might be thinking as she followed me into the living room with Dad close behind.

Having Tina and Ashia in contact with Dad had been helpful at times over the years because he had told them things that Mum and I would otherwise not have known. At one stage he told Tina that Abdul Khada, the man who believed he was my father-in-law, had come to Britain with some documents to take me back to Yemen after I escaped. Mum and I both laughed when we heard that. We would like to see him turn up on either of our doorsteps to try to enforce that. He hasn't yet plucked up the courage to face us. After eight years of being terrorised and tortured by Abdul Khada in Yemen, I would like a chance to get my hands on him in Britain.

But, even as we were laughing, we both felt a tremor of apprehension. Who would have believed that Dad would have been able to arrange for Nadia and me to be sold when we were fourteen and fifteen? It was never a good idea to underestimate the powers of men like Dad and Abdul Khada. So it had been useful to know what they were planning.

Dad's wife was sitting in the living room as I strode in. I glanced at her but said nothing and sat myself down on the settee. She looked young and her eyes were wide with fear and confusion. She must have wondered what was going on. God knows what stories she had heard about me from Dad and his cronies. She had probably been told that I was mad and dangerous, some sort of devil woman who was determined to ruin their lives. I guess in many ways I was. There were two small children playing on the floor and I could see she was pregnant with a third. The children didn't come near me. I guess they could sense that I hadn't come as a friend. I doubt if they realised I was their big sister.

As I sat, staring at them silently while Dad and Tina talked, I felt sorry for them. They might live in Birmingham, but they were cut off from their own family who lived only a few streets away. They had no idea who Liam and Cyan and Mark were. In fact these little children were my kids' uncle and aunt. I thought how sad it was that they couldn't be part of our extended family network, playing together naturally every day.

I guess, once they are a little older, Dad will send them off to Yemen to be married or join the army and we will never see them again. It would be nice to think that one day they might come looking for us, to find out about their half-brothers and sisters, but they probably won't. Since his wife is a Yemeni herself, she would have no problem going back with them. She would never end up in the terrible situation that Mum has found herself in.

I would have loved to have been involved in their lives, but I knew I never could be because it would mean being involved with Dad again. If he was to die or disappear then I would start to visit them and try to help them in any way I could, but it is unthinkable while he is living with them.

Tina explained to Dad that I was there because Mo was in Yemen and I wanted to take any phone calls that came in from him.

Dad didn't protest. He seemed quite humble, trying to make normal conversation to Tina despite the fact that his voice was cracking with emotion. My silent, sullen presence must have unnerved him. He must have been able to feel how I hated him and how close I was to attacking him. The atmosphere in the room was thick with tension.

He hadn't changed much since I had last seen him, just got older, with a lot more grey hair. None of us know for sure how old he is because he lied about his age when he first came to England, and has continued to change it to suit the circumstances ever since. I couldn't believe that such an insignificant little man could still have so much control over our lives. We had had nothing to do with him for years, and yet he could still keep Nadia away from us. He could still keep my son Marcus away from me. He could still ensure that Nadia's children never got to know their maternal family.

I was an adult woman, living in a supposedly free society, and he was still able to control my family as if I was a small child. Yet he had abused every paternal privilege possible and shown himself to have no one's interests at heart except his own. He had never done a single thing for any of us. He had been content to destroy the lives which Mum had managed to build for us. I hated him so much at that moment that I ached to pick up a knife and slit his throat.

Everything that I had been through in Yemen came back to me as I listened to his voice. I remembered the beatings and the humiliations, the rapes and the untreated illnesses. I thought of Marcus and how I had been made to leave him behind in order to escape, and I thought of Nadia, still there after all those years.

When he realised that I was serious and did not intend to leave until he had made an arrangement for me to talk to Nadia and Mo, Dad picked up the phone and dialled Nasser Saleh's number. Without a word I took the phone off him and put it to my ear. It was ringing.

'Hello.' Nadia's voice came on the line. By some fluke she had picked up the ringing phone herself. It seemed ridiculously easy after all this time. I was taken aback to find myself talking to her so quickly. I had expected Dad and Nasser Saleh to keep me running around with delaying tactics for at least a couple of weeks before I was finally able to get through. I tried to think what to say.

'Hello,' I said. 'Do you know who this is?'

'Yeah,' she said as casually as if I had seen her just the day before.

The tension in the room in England meant that I couldn't talk to her properly, knowing that Dad was listening to every word, willing me to say something that he would be able to use against me at a later date. I asked if Mo was doing all right and she said he was.

'How are you feeling inside?' I asked.

'I was just telling Mo,' she replied.

She spoke in English all the way through the conversation, never lapsing into Arabic, which was amazing because even after ten years back in England I still break into Arabic occasionally, especially when I'm shouting at the kids. I guess she had been talking to Mo when the phone rang and had got back into the habit of speaking English.

When I had finished talking to her I passed the phone to Tina. I walked straight out to the car without looking at Dad, and waited for her to follow. Once I was out of the house I was in no hurry to get home. I needed time to sort my thoughts out. When Tina finally climbed in beside me neither of us spoke. We drove back to Mum's house in a deafening silence.

We told Mum what had happened and from then on Tina and I never spoke to one another about the events of that day again. It was as if neither of us wanted to have to admit out loud that that man was actually our father.

Tina told Mum she had asked Nadia if she was going to come back to England with Mo.

'I can't,' Nadia had said. 'Mohammed has put the kids into school and there's not another holiday coming up now until June. We will be coming over soon. Mohammed has promised me.'

I remembered those sorts of promises. When I had been out there with her they had always been promising that we would be able to go back to England 'when the time was right', but the time never was right. I was amazed that she still believed anything they told her, but I suppose if she doesn't grasp the little straws of hope which they hold out to her then she has nothing else left. She has to believe that one day they will let her go, otherwise there would be no point in going on.

I felt sure, as soon as Tina told Mum about the school excuse, that Nadia wasn't going to be coming back with Mo. It was all another set-up by Mohammed and his family. More excuses. More complications. More lies. More hopelessness.

Another phone call was set up from Dad's house for me to speak to Mo a few days later. It was a difficult conversation. I guessed that there were other people in the room with Mo and he was trying to give me coded messages. It was impossible for either of us to speak freely about what might be happening in those dingy rooms in Taiz.

Once he was down there, Mo sent us regular faxes to let us

know what was going on. He told us that Mohammed now had a job as a policeman in a town called Hodeidah, which was about four hours' drive from Taiz, but that he had taken time off to be with Nadia when she met her brother. That came as no surprise to any of us. We hardly imagined that he would trust his wife to be talking with her family unchaperoned after all this time. He made sure that he came to see Mo soon after his arrival. I guess he wanted to make sure that Mo knew he was around and in charge.

'I brought the tickets for all of you,' Mo told Mohammed. 'Shall we go to the British embassy and get the passports for the children, so that we can all travel back to England together?'

'Tickets?' Mohammed looked surprised and then angry. 'I didn't want you to bring the tickets. I wanted you to bring the money.'

Nadia looked at him in horror and then burst into tears. 'You promised me,' she shouted at Mohammed and ran from the room.

Despite this, Mo seemed to be optimistic about Nadia's attitude and his chances of persuading her to come home once Mohammed had gone back to work and left them together. I began to wonder if I had misjudged the situation and there was some hope after all.

After three days the cheery tone of the early faxes changed. A hint of panic seemed to be creeping into Mo's words. 'She's stubborn, Mum,' he wrote. 'It's not working out the way I wanted it to. They're putting pressure on us.'

Mum and I began to feel scared for him. I could imagine

how hard it must have been for Mo, trying to tell Nadia everything that the family had been doing over the last ten years, attempting to inspire her with the will to try to get free. He would not have understood the way Nadia's mind works in the same way that I would have done. She would have been far more reserved about her emotions with him. She wouldn't have let him past the tough exterior shell which she has developed over the years to protect herself from the constant disappointments and the daily struggle to keep going.

10

'Well, She Said It, Didn't She?'

Life in Taiz was much easier for Mo than it had ever been for Mum or Jana, simply because he was a man. In Yemen life is for the men and the women are only there to serve them and have their children.

Mo was free to come and go from the house where he was staying. He didn't have to answer to anyone. He didn't find 'taxi drivers' or 'guides' popping up at every corner, insisting on taking care of him as Mum had. He was able to melt discreetly into the background of coffee shops and marketplaces, able to pass along the busy streets without anyone giving him a second look.

Nick and his team, who were also in the city, were able to meet him and surreptitiously film him in the street without anyone noticing. They needed background footage to complement the fuzzy audio tapes which Mo was making of his conversations with Nadia. They wanted to show the contrast between Taiz and Birmingham, to give an idea of how wide the cultural gap was into which Nadia and I had fallen.

When he came back to England, Mo brought with him a ninety-minute tape. I had mixed feelings about listening to it. I desperately wanted to hear Nadia's voice, but I knew that the sound of it would break my heart. I would feel terrible if she talked about how bad her life was, and equally terrible if she claimed she was happy, because I would know that she was still being forced to lie. I plucked up my courage and agreed to listen.

As we heard the familiar tones of her voice we could understand how things had started to go wrong between her and Mo. At the beginning she was really relaxed and comfortable. She sounded confident and pleased to have a member of the family come out to see her.

When Mo asked her about the past she said she didn't want to talk about it. I can imagine how painful it must be for her to remember everything she has been put through. I'm sure that the day she arrived in Yemen is burned indelibly into her memory. It certainly is in mine. The men made me tell her that she had been married to a boy she had never met, and would not be going back to Birmingham. That moment must come back to her in her worst nightmares when she is having to lie beside Mohammed and listen to his snoring.

Going through the suitcase of presents that we had sent out with Mo must have been very emotional for her. When you live in such a different world, stripped of comfort, the sight of something as simple as a favourite brand of crisps can bring all sorts of memories flooding back. As she went through the different things she talked to Mo about each item, like an excited schoolchild opening her Christmas stocking.

I can still remember the dry, powdery taste of the chocolates and biscuits that she and I used to buy in Yemen when we had managed to get hold of a little money and were trying to cheer ourselves up with a tiny luxury. When she tasted Toffos again it must have reminded her of our childhood together, when she was never to be seen anywhere without a packet of them about her somewhere.

'Where's my family?' she asked Mo at one moment on the tape. 'I want to go home.'

But when she spotted the tape recorder we could hear the panic in her voice. 'Turn it off!' she said. 'Don't do this to me. I'll get into trouble.'

Mo kept the tape running.

The moment she thought that her words might be reported in the media and would get back to her husband, Nadia began spouting the same robotic lines we had heard before in front of the television cameras. She said how happy she was and how she didn't want to leave Yemen.

From the cheerful, sisterly chat, she went back to talking like an alien. Her voice became angry and bitter towards Mo, as if he was the instrument of her unhappiness. Perhaps at that instant she thought he was. Even though she now knew Mo had taped her talking about wanting to come home earlier, she denied everything.

When Mo finally agreed to turn the tape recorder off she told him how much pressure she had had to suffer when Mum and Jana had been out there, and whenever delegates from the British embassy decided to pay visits to the village.

'They all scare me,' she said. 'Even the people from the embassy told me that if I wanted to return to England I would have to leave the children behind. I couldn't bear to do that. Who would look after them if I wasn't here? I have to do whatever they tell me. When they put a letter in front of me and tell me to copy it I have to do it.'

We already knew this was true because in one letter Mum had received from her she had signed off 'Yours faithfully', and throughout the text her spelling and punctuation had been perfect. We knew that Nadia couldn't spell when she was fourteen and still at school in England. Having been in Yemen for sixteen years, speaking Arabic every day and reading virtually nothing in any language, she was hardly likely to have improved her writing style.

'If it was your choice,' Mo said to her at one stage on the tape, 'what would you want to do?'

'I don't know what you mean,' she said, sounding genuinely puzzled by the idea of being able to make a choice for herself.

'If you were the man and you could choose to do whatever you wanted,' he explained patiently. 'What would you choose to do?'

'I would travel,' she said.

'Travel where?'

'Travel everywhere.'

I knew exactly what she meant because I felt the same when I first escaped. I wanted to travel all over the world and I've been able to do it because of the promotions for the book. I know how trapped I felt being in Yemen for eight years. Still to be there nearly ten years later would have driven me mad.

'But where would you like to go?' Mo persisted.

'Well, where's my home? Where's my family?' she asked. 'England.'

Never, in all the years that different people have been interviewing her, has Nadia ever said that she doesn't want to come back to England. She sometimes says, 'It's impossible,' and she sometimes says, 'Don't worry Mum, I'm all right.' She even says Mohammed is a good husband to her sometimes – when he is listening. But she never says that she doesn't want to come back. We know that she would say it if she felt it, because then all the pressure would be taken off her. If we heard her say it and we believed she meant it, we would stop trying to fight for her release and we would leave her to live the life of her choice in the village. But we know that is not the case.

All this was on the tapes. When we played them to Nick he asked which parts we wanted him to use in the film. We begged him to let the public hear her saying that she wanted to travel and to come to England to see her family. Those words summed up the dreams we knew she held in her heart. We asked him not to play the parts in which she reverted to talking like a robot, spouting the lines that she had been intimidated into repeating about being happy where she was and wanting to be left alone.

We explained to him that when she talked in that robot-like voice it was because she had gone inside her shell. She has been in Yemen nearly twenty years. Since I left she has had no one to talk to about her feelings, no one she can completely trust.

She has had no way of relieving the tensions. So she bottles everything up to stop herself from running screaming into the mountains, or attacking someone with a carving knife.

Instead, she sits alone like a dead-eyed zombie, mouthing the lines which she thinks will make people leave her alone. It is like a dog which has grown used to being beaten every time it barks or shows any high spirits. Eventually, the poor animal will stop trying and will slink away into a corner, concentrating on doing nothing to upset its tormentors or draw attention to itself.

When Nadia shows her bitterness towards Mum or me or Mo it is because she knows that whenever we go to see her, we will leave her again. I remember when Mum first came out to find us, and then had to go back to England in order to continue the fight for our freedom. It was almost impossible to bear the pain of seeing her go, knowing that we were being abandoned yet again. We knew there was nothing else she could do, but that didn't stop the feelings of emptiness and betrayal. Each time one of us goes down to try to reach her, Nadia suffers that loss over and over again.

If you are constantly disappointed, you eventually stop being hopeful. I also think that Nadia tells people she is all right and happy because she doesn't want Mum to worry. She is putting on a brave face, but we can tell from the way she says these words that they are not coming from inside her. They are just the learned responses of someone who is tired of having her hopes raised and dashed.

We explained all this to Nick. He promised us that he would use the quotes which showed her real feelings – the moments when she opened up to Mo and told him what she really wanted – and we trusted him.

Initially, Mo was only supposed to stay in Taiz for a week. He extended his visit for another three days in the hope that if he spent some more time with Nadia he would be able to penetrate her reserve. He hoped to help her remember who she really was and what she really wanted from life.

The whole experience shocked him deeply. Perhaps he had allowed himself to become too optimistic about his chances of success. When he found that he actually couldn't help Nadia any more than Mum or I could, the disappointment hit him hard. Seeing someone you love suffer, and being unable to ease their pain, is one of the worst experiences anyone can go through.

When he arrived back in England he found it hard to talk about anything that he had seen or experienced in Yemen. It was as if he needed time to digest it and understand what it all meant. I know there were things that he decided not to tell me for fear that he would upset me too much, and I didn't want to push him. He had taken some pictures of Nadia and the children and I was shocked by how thin and old she had become. Whilst her children all looked robust and happy, she seemed to have had the life sucked out of her. Tina has grown to be beautiful and looks exactly like her mother. Seeing her serene face in the pictures reminds us of the Nadia we used to know all those years ago in England.

Mo told me little things, not always realising how significant they were to me. When he told me that Mohammed had complained to him about how the kids always clung to Nadia in the village, I knew that meant Nadia had not really changed. Most of the local women of the villages push their children away from them at the first opportunity. Perhaps they do it because they know that they are going to be taken from them and they don't want to make the bonds too tight; or perhaps it is because they simply don't have the time or energy to spare for them. Nadia, however, still behaves like a British mother, trying to protect and nurture her children for as long as possible. That would also explain why she looks so much more exhausted and drained than the other village women. She gives too much of herself to the children.

On his return, Mo wanted to spend a lot of time alone. He would disappear up into the attic on his own for hours on end. When he came down his knuckles would be bleeding and bruised. None of us liked to ask why. There was a look in his eyes which discouraged us from asking any personal questions or attempting to pry behind the mask which he had constructed.

One day, when he was out, Mum and I went up to see what he did up there. We could see the indentations of his fist marks where he had been punching the walls, inflicting pain on himself as if trying to physically force out the bad thoughts. Perhaps he imagined that the walls he was punching were actually Dad's and Mohammed's faces?

His girlfriend told us that he was having difficulty sleeping at night. He would often give up trying, getting up at two or three in the morning. He would go out for long walks and not come back for hours. I could imagine the feeling of wanting to clear his head of all the ugly pictures which had been put there by whatever Nadia had told him. But I know that it is impossible to do that. All you can do is distract yourself with other things.

If I keep myself busy I can push the pictures of Yemen to the back of my mind for short periods, but they always come back. I can make myself not think about all the wasted years when I am rushing around during the day. But if I can't get to sleep at night it is impossible to stop it all flooding back and it's made a hundred times worse by tiredness. Sometimes it is overwhelming.

Mo went to see Gowad before he left Birmingham, to ask why Nadia and Mohammed and the kids couldn't come to England just for a holiday. In families like Gowad's, respect for the father is absolute. Mohammed would never do anything unless his father had approved it, even though he is a grown man himself. (No doubt Dad hoped that by sending us to Yemen we would learn to respect him without question as well. While I was living in Mokbana, confused and partly brainwashed, I almost became the sort of daughter he wanted me to be. I guess Nadia has fulfilled his ambitions in that respect by giving in to the wishes of the men in her life.) Mo knew that if he could persuade Gowad to give his permission Nadia and her children could be on a plane within a few days.

Gowad pretty much laughed in Mo's face. I can imagine how he must have dismissed my brother as little more than a naïve boy who should know better than to question the wisdom of his elders and betters. I imagine Gowad was probably nervous of Mo, and that made him all the more patronising.

The fury and frustration that Mo had bottled up against the man who held the power to make everything in our sister's life come right, exploded and he ran amok. As he left the house he grabbed bricks and hurled them back through Gowad's windows. It probably helped Mo to let off that steam, but it cost him dearly. Gowad went to the police and Mo ended up in court and was made to pay for the damage.

It seems to me that we live in a strange world of distorted priorities when a man who continues to perpetrate such terrible crimes against other people can demand recompense for a few broken windows and be given it. The authorities are happy to intervene when property is damaged but are apparently powerless to act when a young girl is continually being damaged, year after year.

My relationship with Mo is stronger now than it has ever been. Having been out there and glimpsed inside Nadia's life he understands exactly what Mum and I have been through and it has changed him completely. Anything I say to him, I know that he understands. We can sit together for hours in silence and we both know what the other one is thinking. He is trying to get back to leading a normal happy life, just as we all are, but the shadows are always there in the back of his mind. Even if Nadia came home tomorrow, I don't think anyone could ever completely undo the damage which has been done to us all by the last twenty years.

Mo managed to get hold of a picture of Marcus. His father's family must have heard through the grapevine that Mo was visiting and sent the picture to him via Nadia. Now I have a snapshot of my first son. He is nearly ten years older than when I last saw him. I know nothing else about him. I don't know who his friends are or what his favourite foods are. I don't know if he is a kind boy or a bully. I don't know if he is clever at school or not. Does he show off when he is at home, or quietly go about his chores? There is no one to tell me any of these things. Although we received reports via the British embassy that he was with Nadia at various times, none of them was true. Nadia claims that she hasn't seen him since I left.

However hard I stare at the picture I can't recognise the child I left behind. He has become all grown up, wearing a flowing white robe and a headdress like Yasser Arafat's. There is a dagger at his waist. He is a young man, old enough now to drive a car in the Yemen, or go to work in any one of a number of Arab countries.

I wonder, as I stare at the picture, if he gets to mix with his cousins in Ashube. Has he been told the tale about the two 'sad sisters of the Mokbana' as Nadia and I were called at the time?

With all the international publicity it seems likely that our story is still talked about by the women when they are doing their washing or cooking and the men as they sit in the shade chewing quat and discussing the world. I'm sure someone would have brought copies of either *Sold* or *Without Mercy* into the area after picking them up at an airport or receiving them from a relative in England.

Not much happens in the Mokbana. Life is monotonous and the days are long. People tell stories to pass the time, and I can't believe that Marcus wouldn't have overheard something that would have made him curious to find out more. At school his friends must know at least some of the truth. I hope they are kind and don't taunt him with it.

I try to look behind the picture to see if I can see the little baby that I had to leave behind but I can't see him. I have lost all the years between and there is no way I can get them back. When I look at the picture I see a stranger. I have no way of knowing how long it will be before I actually meet him again. Perhaps I never will. Thinking about it makes my head hurt and brings the tears back again.

I remember how he used to cling to me all the time when he was tiny, and I wonder what happened to him after I went. I would have been a good, loving mother to him but circumstances wouldn't allow it. He has been left to be brought up with an empty space in his heart, missing the one person who should have been with him. But as far as the British and Yemeni governments are concerned it is an unimportant detail. Every time they delayed a decision for another year they took away a year of Marcus's childhood.

In my lowest moments after Mo came back I told myself that maybe Nick Gray's film would change everything. Maybe it would cause another political stir and someone in power would find a way for Marcus and me to be together again. I had to put my faith in him.

After coming back from Yemen, Nick sat us down round the table at home and filmed us giving our opinions of what Nadia must be going through, judging from the tapes we had heard. He was being so thorough with the preparation for the programme that I was growing more and more optimistic about the impact it would have once it was shown.

He also travelled back and forth to America a few times. He managed to track down Don and Judy Feeney from CTU and interviewed them about their line of work. He didn't tell them that he was involved with us, just that he had been in touch with some mums who had worked with them and he was interested in what they did to help people. They must have been thrilled at the idea of getting some free publicity on British television.

He brought up Mum's name in conversation with them and they were as plausible and confident as they had always been. They said that our chances of success had always been low, but they didn't say anything about giving us a refund if they were unsuccessful. When Nick pressed harder about the money, Judy turned and walked out of the interview. The footage, and Nick's line of questioning, made it clear to the viewer that he thought they had ripped us off.

Once we started to talk in public about how much money we had given the Americans with no results, other mums contacted us to say that they had had the same experience. Some of them were women that Mum had met over the years on television programmes about snatched children, or at meetings of Reunite and other organisations. None of them had lost as much money as we had; either they had realised earlier what was happening or they simply hadn't had access to such large sums in the first place.

Our biggest mistake had been keeping quiet for so long about what we believed the Americans were doing for us. If

Mum had talked about them at any of the meetings she had attended, someone would have warned her much earlier that they did not always deliver on their promises. We would not then have gone on giving them money for so long. By the time we found this out it was too late for us to do anything about it. But then the secrecy and discretion had all been at their insistence, so it was not surprising that it worked in their favour.

One of the daytime television shows actually persuaded one of the CTU men to appear and answer the allegations which we and other dissatisfied clients were making. He had his face screened out so that no one would be able to recognise him. His defence was that there were never any certainties in his business. He said that there was always a chance that they wouldn't be able to pull off any job and that they always explained this risk to the families.

I remember at our early meetings, they told us there was an 80–90 per cent chance of success. I had started out believing it was probably more like 50 per cent, until I saw how professional their plans looked and how much hardware they intended to use. I became more optimistic for a while. I think if they had actually attempted the operation they might well have succeeded. But why would they put themselves to all that trouble? They already had our money.

One of the men who worked for them left and set up a company of his own. He rang Mum to ask if she knew of any other mothers with whom they could get in touch. Mum suggested that he get Nadia and the children out and then she would be happy to recommend him to everyone.

Nick had decided that in the interests of fairness he should give Dad a chance to tell his side of the story. He went to see him early in the research process, and listened to all the same stuff that Dad had been spouting for nearly twenty years about how he had only wanted to save us from the sinful ways of modern Britain and teach us how to be good Arab women and followers of the Koran.

After returning from Taiz and learning more about the situation, Nick decided that he should see Dad again. I didn't mind because I knew that Dad was never able to give journalists any convincing arguments to justify his actions. He usually ended up ranting and raving at them and making it obvious that he had no moral defence.

'What do you want now?' Dad shouted at Nick when he knocked on the door.

'Just to find out what has happened to Nadia since we left Taiz,' Nick said innocently.

'Nadia's back in her village now,' Dad yelled. 'She is under the protection of her family.'

I could believe that. I knew they wouldn't want her to stay in Taiz longer than was strictly necessary. Women who live in cities tend to become more Westernised and self-confident, less easy to intimidate and brainwash. So we knew that he was telling the truth and that Nadia was back in the mountains, waiting for whatever might befall her next.

When he had put the film together Nick brought the final rough cut for us to watch at home. I cried all over again as I heard Nadia's voice and listened to the rest of us talking about her.

Cyan was sitting on my lap, watching with us. She saw me crying on the screen and turned to look at me for reassurance. She saw the real tears which I was unable to keep from springing into my eyes and her face wrinkled with concern.

'Grandad's horrible, isn't he?' she said. 'He won't let Auntie Nadia home.'

'What are you crying for, Cyan?' I asked, my voice gruff with emotion.

'Nothing,' she said, quickly. 'My eyes are just watering.'

I wished I hadn't let her watch the programme. I didn't want her to have to see her mother cry.

The film was wonderful. Nick had done a great job – until it came to the bit about whether Nadia wanted to stay or come out. I couldn't believe, as I sat listening to the soundtrack, that he had done exactly the opposite of what we had asked. He had used the bit of the tape where she was saying she was happy and didn't want to leave, and had cut out the bit about wanting to travel and see her family. At the last moment it seemed that he had chickened out and taken the opposite side to us – or perhaps he had been directed to do so.

As I heard the words coming out of the television I felt as if I had been punched in the stomach. I couldn't believe what I was hearing. I felt that once again we had been let down. Anyone watching the film would be left with the impression that although the story had been a great tragedy, Nadia had now come to terms with her life out there and that there was no point in going on with our campaign to get her free.

The time had come, the viewer would be bound to

conclude, for us to give up and accept that we had lost the struggle. Neither Mum nor I were about to do that. Nick's film was going to end up working against our cause, not for it.

We exchanged angry words with Nick, and I later told him in a letter that his problem was that he didn't know what love was because he had never had children.

The documentary, screened in spring 1997, was moderately successful and they managed to sell the rights to Spain. Despite our reservations Mum and I went to Barcelona with Nick to promote it. We were due to appear together on a chat show after it had been screened. If there was any chance of putting our story across again in a few more newspapers in a few more countries, I was going to be there. Nick's film might not have helped us by showing what Nadia truly felt, but it was providing us with another platform to tell our story to the public and stir up some controversy.

I didn't talk to Nick all the way down to Spain. He knew how I felt and he knew I was developing a reputation for being a bit of a hard case – someone who didn't care who she upset. He avoided my gaze and I felt sure that he was feeling pangs of guilt, but that was no consolation to me.

When the television company in Spain asked me on to a programme to talk about the film after the broadcast, I explained the sort of emotional state which I knew Nadia would be in after so much time. I was determined to do everything I could to undermine the impression that the film had left in viewers' minds.

We received a lot of publicity in Spain, but in Britain the response to the documentary, which was seen by about three million people, was very disappointing. I think Yorkshire Television received two or three letters on the subject, but it was nothing like the response we got from the book. It was a terrible disappointment. We felt that if we wanted to get the full story told on television we would have to start all over again with another documentary team. The thought of having to go through months of interviews again was almost too much to bear.

I suppose we shouldn't have been surprised by the lack of response in England. We have never been able to stir up the passions of the British public in quite the same way as we have in Europe. In countries like France and Holland, everyone seems to be outraged by what has happened to us. Everyone from the governments to the publishers and journalists wants to do something about it. In Britain everyone seems to have reasons why they shouldn't get involved and why we should let sleeping dogs lie. Nick's only defence for the bits of tape he used was: 'Well, she said it, didn't she?'

When we got back from Spain, Nick went on coming round to visit Mum and trying to remain friendly. I became increasingly irritated. One day I dropped in to see Mum and he was in the kitchen talking to her. I'd had enough and I stormed in with all guns blazing. I accused him of distorting our case for his own greed. I told him we would be making another documentary soon and it would be a lot fairer and better than his. I told him everything was his fault. I can't remember everything else I said now but none of it was complimentary. I was raging round the room and he was sweating and squirming.

'Zana,' he said when I finally let him get a word in, 'I'm really, really sorry. You have no idea how much guilt I'm carrying inside.' I could see from looking in his eyes that he was telling the truth. 'If there is anything I can do to put things right . . .'

'There is nothing you can do,' I snapped. 'Just go away.'

I've heard that his film has been going out in other countries, but we haven't heard from him again.

11

Friends in High Places?

After the documentary had been shown, Jana moved away from Birmingham to the Peterborough area. For a while she lived in a village called Wisbech, which was once the home of a man called Thomas Clarkson, one of the prime movers in abolishing slavery in Britain. There is a bridge built in his memory which is called 'Freedom Bridge'. Moving away from Birmingham did not mean that Jana lost touch with Mum. Mum travelled frequently to Wisbech.

Mum was introduced to a group of solicitors who specialise in human rights cases and who were moved by our story. They asked if they could do anything to help our cause. We jumped at the offer. We had had a number of solicitors and lawyers working for us over the years, to see if we could bring a case against Dad and the other men. We knew how expensive and time-consuming it was to go to the law about anything. We were pretty sure that there must be some legal way of getting Nadia and the children back if we just knew where to look. We could no longer afford to pay a professional solicitor the amounts that would be needed for such a mammoth task. Jana knew all this.

She asked the Wisbech solicitors if they would be willing to look into the legal side of the story for us without charging us. She explained that we had no money left now. They agreed and now have all our documents and are looking to see if they can build a case for us against the British government and everyone else who has been involved in stopping us getting Nadia's basic human rights restored to her.

We still feel, more strongly than we can easily put into words, that freeing Nadia is the responsibility of the British government. It was their responsibility when she was fourteen and should still have been attending school in Birmingham. Because they did not take action quickly, the situation has become much more complicated, and it is now a hundred times harder to arrange for her release because she has six children and has lived in Yemen for so long.

So many people in powerful positions have told us that they will help, and then have given up as soon as they realised how hard a struggle it was going to be, that we have come to believe that there is no basic justice available to us.

All of these people seem to hope that if they just ignore us for long enough we will give up the struggle and stop complaining. That is what happens in most of the families that encounter these sorts of problems, they simply become ground down by the hopelessness of the situation. Mothers who have had their children taken from them end up deciding that it would be better to let them live in peace in slavery than to continue upsetting people by fighting to free them. Neither Mum nor I are willing to give up that easily – ever.

Because of the history of the Wisbech area there are a number of people interested in the questions of slavery and freedom. They are not people in positions of power or influence but they are people with strong beliefs in what is right and what is wrong, people who are willing to give their time and energy to fighting for a cause which they think is right.

Jana arranged to meet some of them and talked to them about our situation. A group of them started to talk about the possibility of creating a concerted campaign to have Nadia freed. Their main aim was to give Mum support and ease some of the pressures on her. They started writing to MPs and anyone else who might have any influence on the case at all.

One member of the group wrote a play about slavery and we went across for a couple of days to listen to a reading. Like so many of these sorts of campaigns there was no money. Everything had to be done in people's spare time on the strength of their goodwill and their convictions that there were wrongs which still needed to be righted.

They gave a private screening of Nick Gray's documentary, which we then had to sit through again. I was surprised by just how shocked the audience was by what they saw. Like most people in the West they had no idea how widespread slavery still is in the world today. There were gasps of surprise throughout the programme. I felt encouraged. Sometimes during our years of struggle I have wondered if we are the only people in the world who felt so strongly that Nadia's situation is wrong. It was a relief to find that these people shared our views.

When we have meetings with them we try to decide who would be the best people for us to get in touch with. Should we, for instance, try to contact Oprah Winfrey and make her aware of our plight, in the hope that she would build a show around us? Should we get in touch with Steven Spielberg because of his interest in the whole subject of slavery? Which television chat show hosts in Europe should we try to contact?

At the same time Jana has also been working on the Internet, going out through her computer looking for people who might have an interest in our case and telling our story to everyone who will listen. The web provides a wonderful opportunity for us to spread the message to places the book hasn't reached. People are responding positively to our message all the time and we are building a bigger and bigger following, but we still can't find anyone who is able to actually get Nadia back. If we were going to wait until the groundswell of opinion grew so great that the government was forced to act, we would all be too old to benefit from the results.

At one of these meetings someone suggested that we should write to Terry Waite and John McCarthy, who were the Beirut hostages with the highest profiles in Britain. Terry Waite was also a well-known Christian with a lot of contacts amongst senior church and political figures. He had been an adviser to both an Archbishop of Canterbury and the Roman Catholic Church and had worked a great deal on international charitable projects before being captured.

We felt sure that, of all people, the Beirut hostages would

understand the concept of innocent people being imprisoned. If we made contact with them they would be able to help us bring our case to the attention of even more influential people.

Jana managed to get hold of Terry Waite's e-mail address and wrote him a letter. A couple of weeks later he wrote back saying that he would be very interested to talk to us. I couldn't believe we were actually going to meet him. I had followed his case on the television, like millions of other people, during the years that the world was campaigning for his release. His big, bearded figure had been one of the most familiar images on the world's news programmes for years.

I remember watching when he was finally released and crying, even though he was a grown man and I had never met him. Whenever I hear any stories about anyone who has been unjustly imprisoned being freed I can't help weeping. The slightest thing stirs up all the emotions which I try to keep under control so that I can continue with my daily life. Once they have been brought to the surface I find the pain almost unbearable. I could imagine exactly what sort of torment he must have gone through during his years of captivity and I felt sure that when we met we would be able to understand one another immediately, two very different people who had shared a similar experience.

An appointment was made and I travelled to Cambridge with Jana and Emile, a man who had been instrumental in helping Jana with our campaign, to meet Terry Waite in a hotel. I was as excited as a child, unable to believe that I was going to be talking face to face with such a monumental historical figure.

As he walked towards us across the hotel foyer I felt a whirl-wind of emotions rising up from the pit of my stomach, clawing at the back of my throat, making it hard for me to get the words out. I was afraid I was going to burst out crying the moment I shook his hand. With a huge effort I forced the tears back down and smiled.

He sat down with us and listened as we went through the story once again. He was so calm and confident. He didn't say much and when he did speak it was in short sentences. He told us that he was familiar with our case and let Jana do the talking.

As I sat, half listening to the familiar story Jana was telling and half watching Terry Waite's reactions, I realised that his case had been very different from ours. He hadn't been dependent on publicity to draw his case to the attention of powerful people. He had already known powerful and influential people and that was why his campaign had succeeded. Because he was already a high-profile figure the media coverage and campaigns automatically followed. As soon as he was captured his story hit the headlines, whereas it had taken six years before the British media realised that Nadia and I had gone missing.

We had no contacts or influence in political circles. The people who had fought for us, people like Mum and Jana and Emile, were almost as helpless as we were. They banged on doors and begged people to listen to what they had to say. All we could do was keep knocking on new doors and telling our story. I realised that if this man decided to join our team and help us to fight we might well get Nadia out. He was in a completely different league and I felt the excitement building inside me. He was personal friends with Robin Cook, after all, who by then had become Foreign Secretary in the Labour government. He could bring our battle to the attention of a whole new level of people. Perhaps this time we were actually going to take a big step forward. Perhaps we had found our champion at last.

When he started asking questions about Nadia – how old she was and whether her health was holding up – I felt the emotions swelling up in my throat again and I was unable to stop the tears from coming. I didn't want to talk about such details because if I did it would bring a picture of Nadia into my mind and I would be unable to speak calmly. I wanted it all to stay at a slight distance, just a familiar story that we were retelling, without any undue emotion. I simply wanted him to understand the facts: that Nadia had been forced into marriage and into staying in the Yemen; and that from the beginning the government had done nothing to help us.

'Leave it with me,' he said when he felt we had told him all he needed to know. 'I will talk to the Foreign Office and let you know what can be done.'

Once more I felt myself stepping on to an emotional roller-coaster. Half of me wanted so much to believe that this time it was going to work. But there was another side of me, the side which had suffered so many disappointments and setbacks and couldn't believe that this would be any different. I wanted to feel optimistic, to have faith and belief that this time it would work out, but I was so afraid of having to suffer another disappointment I didn't dare to hope too much. It was like being torn apart all over again.

After the meeting, on the train back to Birmingham, I became more interested in Terry Waite himself and started asking Jana questions. He had been so charismatic, like a real leader. She explained about his past and we talked about other people we might approach who were in similarly influential positions. We felt sure the more big names we could get on our side the better our chances would be. The meeting had left us charged with optimism.

At the same time we knew we needed to get access to as many official documents relating to our case as possible so that we had something concrete to show to the people we were approaching. To do that we were told we needed to make contact with an MP, something we had not done for several years.

We contacted an MP and arranged a meeting. 'One thing we could do,' I suggested at that first meeting, thinking of the plans which CTU had laid for us, 'is hire some legitimate people to go into Yemen and get her out physically.'

'You'll be committing a crime if you kidnap Nadia,' we were warned.

'That's all right,' I said. 'I'll face the consequences of a jail sentence in Britain if it gets Nadia and the children out of their prison in Yemen.'

'*We'd* be committing a crime?' Mum was getting herself in a right state. 'Have you seen the news today?'

'I don't get time to watch the television,' the MP retorted.

'Well, they're reporting that at the British embassy in Jordan hundreds of thousands of pounds have been embezzled. Just like in Sana'a. It's they who seem to be committing the crimes, the civil servants. We've not committed any crimes.'

We should have known better than to expect anything of any politician, I suppose. During the Margaret Thatcher and John Major years I became convinced that we weren't getting anywhere because we were having to deal with a Conservative government, whose politicians would never be interested in the problems of people like us. When Labour came back to power we felt we stood a chance of being heard and getting something done — even though Mum had written to Tony Blair while he was in opposition and he had simply passed her letter on to someone else. There was a general mood in Britain of making a new start and we felt we might be part of that.

'Nadia is a grown woman,' we were told. 'I can't force her to come over here.' It was the same line we had been hearing for years. But Nadia wasn't a grown woman when she was first taken to Yemen. She was still a child, no older than her own eldest son is now.

'She needs medical help,' we explained, over and over again, to no avail. 'If we could just get her to England to a doctor, then we can see whether she chooses to stay. If she has all her children here and she feels secure, and she still says she wants to go back to the Mokbana then we would never stand in her way. But she has to be able to choose freely, which she can't do as long as she is their prisoner and is so far from her own family.'

We were disappointed, but we still had our hopes pinned on Terry Waite. I imagined him moving about discreetly behind the scenes in the corridors of Westminster and Lambeth Palace, patiently explaining our situation to his friends and contacts, gently insisting that they do something to rectify the situation immediately. All we had to do was wait for him to let us know when she would be freed.

When the documentary was screened we felt that, despite the fact Nick had not used the bits of Nadia's tape in which she talked about how she really felt, it would make a good campaigning tool. We gave the MP a copy of the original tape of Nadia talking to Mo, and said that we had had a meeting with Terry Waite. A copy of the tape was sent to him so that he could hear exactly what Nadia had said, not just the bits included in the film. We felt optimistic. It seemed that we were now beginning to get an organised front.

Terry Waite wrote back a few days later, saying that it sounded to him as if Mo was pressuring Nadia into saying that she wanted to come back. He didn't seem to understand that Mo had had to talk to Nadia in the way that he did in order to make her understand the situation. Mo was becoming angry because Nadia wouldn't say into the tape the words which she had said to him before – words which made her feelings clear.

I remembered hearing Terry Waite say in a documentary about his own experiences that while he was imprisoned he had thought everyone had forgotten him. He didn't seem to have made any allowances for how Nadia must have been feeling about all of us after having been in Yemen for nearly twenty years, half the time believing that we had deserted her.

Baroness Symons wrote back from the Foreign Office, using the old formula that Nadia was a 'dual national' and there was nothing they could do to help. When Mum and I read that we felt close to despair. This took us right back to the beginning, when Nadia and I were still children and they used dual nationality as an excuse for doing nothing. Since then we had forced the British government to admit that it wasn't true and that Nadia and her children were fully British. But now they were ignoring this. They had gone back to parroting the same old excuses, despite the fact that both our parents are British citizens.

We went to a Muslim lawyer for a second opinion and he agreed that even in Islamic law Nadia and the children were fully British.

We were told by the MP that the file would have to be closed, and that there was nothing else that could be done. We tried to contact the Muslim lawyer again but he had disappeared, vanished as if someone had done something to frighten him away.

12

'Don't Worry, Mum'

When I first came back to England in 1988, solicitors advised me that I might be able to sue my father for kidnapping and wrongful imprisonment. We included Gowad in the case in the hope that it would pressure him into letting Nadia out. At that stage we still had faith in the British legal system. I believed that everyone would want to help us once they knew the facts. I did not realise how hard it would be to convince people of those facts.

While the case was in progress Dad started writing to Nadia. God alone knows what he said to her, but she wrote to us saying we should stop causing trouble; that our father was a 'good dad' and he was the only one she loved. We found out later that he told her that we had burned down his fish and chip shop, where we had all been living together before going to Yemen, out of spite. He even sent her a picture of the ruin. It was hardly surprising that she was confused by the time Mum and I spoke to her from the French television studio.

Our case came into court once and was then adjourned due to 'lack of evidence'. The fact that I was a witness to the whole affair apparently counted for nothing. I had spent eight years in Mokbana gathering evidence, but my word was not enough. We didn't give up and the lawyers managed to get another hearing fixed. Before the date came round, however, the British government advised us to drop the case against Gowad, as a sign of goodwill towards the Yemeni government. We said that not only would we drop the case, we would be willing to allow the Yemeni government to take all the praise for their co-operation if they would just let Nadia and the children out.

They accepted the deal and we dropped the charges. Our hopes soared. We had finally found a solution which would not force the Yemenis to lose face. Nadia would finally be coming home to us. It then went very quiet. When we eventually managed to get an official reply, we were told that the Yemenis had reneged on their side of the deal. We had been cheated once more.

Still, even after all this time, Mum and I are dismissed by those in authority as hysterical women, whose word can't be trusted. When the *Observer* journalist, Eileen MacDonald, first came out of Yemen and confirmed that everything Mum had been saying was true, the Foreign Office actually said that now they believed it because they had a witness. They admitted they had not believed Mum.

I can only assume that we are not believed because of the colour of our skins. I can think of no other reason why Eileen should be believed and Mum should not.

The twin disappointments of our experiences with the MP and Terry Waite brought back Mum's asthma and she retired to bed, not moving for several days. The pressure had built up around her again. It was as if she had withdrawn from life for a while in order to cope with the stress. Her body had shut down to give itself time to recharge its batteries.

The constant pressure of Mum's life had also proved too much for her husband, Abdul. He had always been very quiet and was not able to tell his problems to anyone, his time being taken up with listening to all Mum's worries and finding his own way in a new country. I know that he was constantly worried about his own mother in Syria, who was sick and couldn't afford medical treatment.

It must all have grown too much for him to cope with because one day, while Mum was out, he left. There were no warnings, he just disappeared and we haven't heard from him since. I can see why he would have preferred to disappear quietly rather than trying to justify himself to Mum and having to witness her confusion and unhappiness. Maybe the whole marriage was just a sham so that he could get to Britain. If that is so he certainly managed to convince Mum that it was true love.

She was horribly upset to lose the person who she had hoped would be there for her to the end, a quiet, reassuring, supportive presence. But it really seemed like just one more problem amongst a hundred others. It was the setbacks in Nadia's case which really got her down. This may be another reason why Abdul left. He could see that until Nadia was free he could never hope to have more than the tiniest slice of

Mum's attention. She was completely desolated by the realisation that neither the MP nor Terry Waite were going to be of any help to us.

'It doesn't matter, Mum,' I tried to console her. 'It just means that these were not the right people. There will always be somebody else to try. We have to start looking again.'

Two other MPs had been asking us to hand our case over to them ever since we told them, so we passed the papers over and went back to waiting once more.

The Wisbech group had not given up either. They had decided to hold a march to try to get some more publicity going. I liked the idea of making a public protest. I had seen how well it worked for other causes. They arranged to have T-shirts printed and it was decided to hold the march in London, where we were more likely to catch the attention of the national media. The organisers made all the necessary preparations, getting permission from the police and finalising the route, which would end in Trafalgar Square. I began to feel excited at the prospect of doing something positive again.

Mo had taken a picture of Nadia in Taiz which showed how exhausted and thin she was. We had hundreds of copies made and wrote a short piece about how she was still in Yemen after all this time. We planned to hand them out to anyone we saw.

Straight after the documentary was filmed we had started to collect signatures for a petition which we eventually intended to hand in to Downing Street. We had been travelling all over Birmingham asking people to sign. I took about a hundred copies into Liam's school and the children all handed them out to their friends to take home to their families.

We wanted to show the government just how great the strength of feeling was on the street. At the time of writing this book we have managed to collect well over a million signatures. The march would give us an opportunity to add to the list and reach a wider audience.

A coach set out from Birmingham early one morning, taking us south for the day. Most of the people were friends and family, many of them brought their children for an outing. Mum, Paul and I took Liam, Cyan and Mark and explained to them what we were doing.

More people were waiting for us in London, so that by the time we set off at ten o'clock, waving our placards, there were about sixty of us. It was only a small demonstration compared to some, but enough to catch the attention of passers-by. At the time I was a little hurt that more people didn't want to support us that day, but I understand that not everyone wants to participate in that sort of activity and maybe we didn't do enough about publicising it.

It was a beautiful, warm day. Almost everyone we handed the leaflets to said they remembered hearing about our case. Nobody was ever in the least reluctant to sign the petition. As always, we found that everyone we spoke to was sympathetic and shocked to find that Nadia was still a prisoner. Nobody outside Yemen or the Foreign Office ever says that they believe she should stay there or that we should give up trying to get her.

It was a great experience for me, talking to different people. It reconfirmed my faith that the general public everywhere in Europe is on our side. One man who came up to me said he worked for the Inland Revenue.

'It was all wrong,' he said, 'what the tax authorities did to you. They went about it all the wrong way. I don't think they should have stopped your royalties the way they did. If I won the lottery I would give you all the money back.'

I thought that was a genuinely sweet thing to say. I hope he keeps buying those lottery tickets.

We couldn't move very fast because of Mum's asthma. The police who escorted us through the streets teased us about how orderly we were. They said we were the quietest marchers they had ever had to supervise. We had a megaphone and as we grew more confident we started shouting out our message: 'Free Nadia! Free Nadia!', hoping to attract more attention. I had a really sore throat and Mum couldn't get her breath, so Paul did most of the yelling for us.

By the time we reached Trafalgar Square we were all hot and sweaty and some of our wilder friends jumped into the fountains to cool off. I wandered around the crowds of foreign visitors, talking to people and getting more signatures. Three tourists came up and asked if I was Zana Muhsen. They said they had read one of the translations of *Sold* and wanted to have their pictures taken with me. At moments like that I feel we are truly getting our message across to the world. And then I remember that we have still not managed to change the situation since the day I left Yemen in 1988.

By the time we got back on the coach at the end of the day we were all shattered. Everyone fell asleep as we headed back up the motorway to home.

We were disappointed by the amount of publicity we received, but it was a useful learning experience for us. We now know that we rushed the organisation of it because we wanted to strike while the memory of the documentary was still fresh in people's minds. The next one we do will be given more planning and it will be more effective.

Mum's health has grown worse and worse over the years. As the stress has increased, so have her ailments. She has bronchitis, asthma and psoriasis. I'm certain that all of them are brought on by the pressure under which she puts herself, the anxieties she feels for her children, and the frustrations which she has to endure with each new setback. She seems to be propped up by the tablets which she has to take and is driven on by her willpower. The weaker her body grows, the more powerful her will becomes.

Her agoraphobia returned and she started to have panic attacks. She starts shaking the moment someone opens the door, hyperventilating and slurring her speech. Now she won't even consider going out of the house unless one of us is there with her. She is completely dependent on us to take her shopping or bring her anything she needs.

When I had the money, I was able to help her by paying her phone bills and buying her tickets to go wherever she needed to go. Now the money has all gone we are back to where we started. For a while she had the phone cut off, which is like a torture for her.

So many people knew her number and used to call all the time. She couldn't even pick up the phone and talk to Jana whenever she wanted to. It all added to the strain on her and I wish that I was able to do more to alleviate it.

The last we heard about CTU was that they were no longer in America, and they had been forced to flee to the Philippines. Now that I look back on that situation I think that they must have started out as a reputable organisation, doing the best that they could for the mothers who hired them. Then the people who founded it retired or gave up and other people moved in who were not as effective. These people, coasting on the reputations of the founders, realised that they had discovered a method of making easy money and they began to get greedy. By the time it came to our turn they had almost given up bothering, just taking the money and producing lots of plans to keep everyone happy.

Every now and then I catch myself thinking, 'Perhaps they will surprise us. Perhaps one day Mum or Jana will call me and say that Nadia is out and waiting to see us.' But those moments are becoming increasingly rare as time continues to slip by.

Sometimes when I go to Mum's house I find her lying down, unable to move so much as a leg or an arm, drained of all energy. When I think what she has put herself through I am amazed that we didn't have to bury her years ago. Then I think how terrible it would be for her and for Nadia if she went before they could be reunited. It can't be that Nadia is meant to come home just to visit her mother in the cemetery.

Despite all the setbacks, and all the waiting, I still have faith that we will win through in the end. We have to, otherwise what has been the point of the whole thing? I know that the majority of ordinary people are behind us, because they tell me so. Over the years there has been so much publicity that my face is pretty well known on the streets of Birmingham. After each new burst of media attention, like Nick Gray's documentary, I find strangers coming up to me and wishing us luck. Sometimes they give me their telephone numbers, telling me to contact them if there is anything they can do.

Ordinary people can see how unjust it all is, but we have no way of mobilising that public feeling into pressure on those who could do something about it. People have their own lives to lead and their own problems to solve. However well-meaning they may be they have no spare time to fight for our cause.

We know that we are far from being the only ones in this situation. In the early days of our publicity campaign we appeared on a television chat show with some mothers who had formed an organisation called Reunite. We talked to five of these women, all of whom had lost their children to Muslim countries. They later went on to make a documentary in which they travelled together to see the children and I heard that most of them have managed to get their kids back.

I read a Foreign Office statistic which said that three children a day, on average, are abducted from Britain. Even if you divide that figure by three it is still shocking and shows just how many people must be suffering in silence, not even able to make as much noise as we have.

It isn't a problem which is unique to England. Everywhere that I have travelled to promote the book I have been told local horror stories of children who have been abducted by their fathers or their mothers, spirited away to other countries and are never seen by their families again. As the world becomes more cosmopolitan and people travel more and more, it is a problem that is likely to increase.

As long as there are mixed marriages there will be culture clashes and as long as there are marriage breakdowns and divorces there are going to be custody battles. In the midst of all this confusion and social change we have to ensure that the children are listened to and are never deprived of their freedoms. No child should ever be put in the position that Nadia now finds herself in.

It seems to me that it is an issue which somehow gets swept under the carpet. When the animal rights protesters want to stop the export of calves they get themselves on the news every night. When the environmentalists want to stop a new motorway being built through a beauty spot they too seem able to command national attention. Why are we not able to draw the same amount of attention to the plight of enslaved children?

Being in the middle of bringing up three small children, I know just how great it is to be with them when they are growing up, and just how much they get from being with their mother. Marcus and I have had all that taken away from us. We have missed all the days and weeks and months that families are supposed to be together. We've missed the mornings when he woke up feeling ill and just wanted cuddling, and the little arguments about chores and homework he should have done, or meals he should have eaten up.

He's missed knowing what it would be like to live with his little brothers and sister. And Liam, Cyan and Mark have missed having a big brother to play with and to fight with and to protect them.

Sometimes I think that as soon as he is old enough Marcus will get on a plane and come and look for me. But then I realise that he may not even know that I exist. His father's family could have told him anything they like about me. They may have said that I died, or that I was some terrible person who abandoned him for my own selfish reasons. I have no way of knowing what he has been told. I can only hope that he will become so curious about who his mother really was that he will start asking questions and someone in the village will tell him the truth about what happened to me when I was his grandfather's prisoner out there. If he ever decides to come looking for me I will have my arms wide open for him.

I realise that I will have to start my relationship from scratch with him now, and I wish with all my heart that he would come to me while he is still young, rather than waiting until he is a fully grown man. But there is nothing I can do about that, apart from keeping on waiting and hoping. I have been dreaming of that reconciliation since the day I left him.

Before Mo went out to Yemen, I gave him pictures of my children in England to carry with him. I hope that Marcus will get to see them some time. I wonder if Nadia stares at them in the same way I stare at the picture of Marcus, trying to see if there is any family resemblance in their happy little faces. Seeing pictures of us all must make her remember our own childhood together. I hope those memories bring her comfort and not just sadness.

She can still remember all her schoolfriends. Even though they are grown up and have children of their own now, she still asks after them on the rare occasions any of us are able to talk to her. She must find it hard to envisage them as adults. None of them have changed as much as she has.

In Birmingham, we live in a close community and we still see each other regularly. When I am with my friends I don't feel as if any of us have changed that much in the twenty years, despite what has happened to us. We still talk and laugh in just the same ways we did when we were kids and we were looking forward to leaving school and going out into the world for adventures.

None of us could ever have imagined then what lay ahead for some of us. All our friends know what happened to Nadia and me, but they never talk about it. They might ask me if I have heard from Nadia every so often, but the answer is nearly always the same and so there is nothing more they can say. We just get on with our lives. I hope that Nadia can see from the photographs that she would be able to fit back into life in England without any trouble.

I like to imagine her sitting down in the evenings in Ashube, when all her chores have been done, looking at the pictures and imagining what life would be like for her if she ever managed to get away. I guess that must be hurtful, but I'm sure she would not want to forget and I want her to keep in mind that we are all still here for her.

I remember how pleased I was when Mum found us six years after we had been taken and showed us pictures of the others. It did make me feel even more homesick than before, but it also strengthened my determination to go on fighting until I was free. I want to keep hope alive in Nadia's heart in the same way, even though I know that for most of the time she must be despairing that we will ever be able to reach her.

Mo told me that Nadia had her four big children with her

in Taiz and that the boys had hung around him like flies, constantly pestering him to play football with them. They all spoke enough English to communicate with him, and they all wanted to come back to Birmingham with him. I guess to them England sounds like an exotic promised land, full of football matches, televisions and chocolate bars. Perhaps Nadia tells them tales of the land she was born in and they know that many of the grown-ups in their lives come here.

Mo asked Nadia about Marcus, but she didn't know anything about him. Although part of me wishes that he could have stayed with her after I left, another part of me is glad that she wasn't burdened with another mouth to feed because of me.

Despite all the media coverage, and all the developments there have been in telephone and satellite communication over the last ten years, the village men are still able to make Nadia disappear from view for years at a time. If she died they would be able to keep the news from us for years, and in my darkest moments I imagine that is what they are doing.

We send her letters, care of Nasser Saleh, but they vanish into the postal system and we have no way of knowing if they reach her. Nothing ever comes back from her and I doubt if anything we send gets any further than Taiz. Perhaps Mohammed opens them and laughs at our inability to defeat him as he reads about our sadness.

Sometimes I think I can hear Nadia's voice in my head, as if we are talking to one another telepathically. It isn't anything dramatic ever. She isn't screaming at me to get her out, we just have normal little everyday conversations. Sometimes I tell myself it is just my imagination and I try to block her out. Then I realise that I want to hear anything that my imagination might want to tell me and so I answer her. She tells me that she knows we are doing the best we can, and encourages us to keep going and not to give up.

The last time Mum or I actually spoke to her was on her birthday in September 1996. Mo had only just come back and we managed to get through to her on the phone in Taiz.

'How old are you, Nard?' I asked.

'I'm thirty one,' she said.

'No you're not, you're thirty two.'

'Yeah?' She sounded surprised.

One of the last things she said to Mum before she disappeared back to the Mokbana again was, 'Don't worry, Mum. Stay calm. Mohammed has promised that we will come to England on holiday soon.'

A promise is a comfort to a fool, but I pray she doesn't realise that. She doesn't know the depths of the corruption which we have encountered every day since we started on this campaign. She still believes that men like Mohammed who read the Koran must be true to their word. Maybe that's a mercy. Maybe that is what helps her to survive from one day to the next.

Mum arranged to ring again a month or so after her birthday. She was told to ring Nasser Saleh's house at an appointed time. We all went to Mum's house so we could talk to Nadia. When everyone was there Mum put the call through.

'She's not here,' came the reply.

'Could you go and get her, please,' Mum asked. We knew that the flat where she would be was only just round the corner from the house.

'Ring back in half an hour,' the voice said.

We did as he asked but received the same answer. We were told to try again in a few hours. We did that and Nasser Saleh said: 'She's in Hodeidah with her husband.'

'When will she be coming back?' Mum asked.

'I don't know,' he said.

We knew then that she had been taken back to the village.

When the Yemeni kidnapping stories became big news in Britain at the beginning of 1999, a BBC television reporter called Peter Wilson used the story as a peg to interview me on the news. He also rang the Foreign Office to enquire if they knew anything about Nadia's whereabouts. He was told that Nadia had been into the embassy to apply for passports for herself and for six children, 'with no intention of travelling'. They said they were also happy for Mohammed to travel to England as a British Overseas Citizen since his father had British citizenship.

When the officials were questioned more closely it became obvious that no one was quite sure whether it was Nadia herself who had come in. They also admitted that the passports had been 'posted' to her. The chances that she would have received them seem remote to me. It is much more likely that the documents have been sold and that someone else is now in Britain on the strength of them.

I have learnt so much over the last ten years and there are many things that I would do differently if I had my chance again. Both Mum and I have made mistakes and we have paid the price in disappointment every time. But I know we have done the best we can at any given moment.

Whenever an opportunity seems to present itself we grab it and put every ounce of energy that we can muster into it. But I never feel that we have done everything we can. I am still certain that if we keep battling on we will find a way to solve our problem.

Every day I wonder if maybe tomorrow something will happen which will change everything. I keep hoping that we will find the right path to the right people.

Maybe it will be this book, and any publicity that we are able to get for it, that will finally make it possible for us to be together again. Maybe someone in a position to help us will read these words and be moved to come forward. Maybe then I will be able to fulfil my promise to Nadia.

Epilogue

P aul knows that the tears routinely overwhelm me. He steps
in to distract the children when he sees that I can't go on.
If it hadn't been for him I don't think I would have got as far
as I have with protecting them from the truth and helping
them to be such happy, carefree little people.

Paul is very supportive. He lets me go off each day and have
my little cry, and my little chat with God. Afterwards I sleep
for a few minutes because the unhappiness drains my energy. If
I haven't managed to ease my pain enough with the crying,
then I will talk to Paul about how I feel. He can never really
understand what I'm talking about, not in the same way as the
family members who have actually been out to Yemen and
experienced what I have experienced.

He hasn't read *Sold* or *Without Mercy*. He hasn't watched the
documentary. I don't think he would be able to bear seeing
how much we actually suffered. A lot of my close friends feel
like that. They know the basic story but they never mention it.

By not talking about it, it is possible to forget it for short periods, and those periods allow us to recharge our batteries for the continuing battles.

I don't want to give the impression that my life is all about sadness and bitterness. I have done many things apart from campaign for Nadia since getting out of Yemen. I have, for instance, taken a lot of courses to equip myself for work.

Paul and I would like to foster children once my career is sorted out. We've been interviewed and inspected and given the go-ahead. I would only want to take on school-age kids, I wouldn't want to deal with babies and infants. I know just how terrible it can be to be separated from your family when you are still young. I want to be able to help kids get over that.

Children who need fostering have often been subjected to tragedy or have experienced loss. They may have been victims of violence or sexual abuse or neglect. They may have had parents who couldn't cope with them. Whatever their stories, I know that I can offer them the love that they need and I want to be as well trained and developed as I can be for the job of trying to repair their emotional lives. I want to be able to give them the chance which I had to live a normal life after their trauma, so that they can avoid ending up as trapped and helpless as Nadia still is, whatever their circumstances might be.

Until recently, the fostering authorities would not have considered a single parent as a foster parent, but now the demand is so great they are actually advertising for people like me. In my dreams I imagine myself living in a mansion somewhere with ten or twenty kids running around. Of course, I wouldn't be doing it on my own. Paul is nearly always at home. He is great with kids and is much more patient than I am. If we had the money we would get married, but I don't want to do it unless we can afford to do it properly. I don't want a big wedding, just close friends and family, but I want it done in a little church with the men in top hat and tails. Maybe one day soon, when we get ourselves straight.

Despite not being able to truly picture what our lives in Yemen were like, Paul listens to me and helps me. He is my therapist. He keeps me sane. He also makes it possible for me to do all the things I have to do in my campaign to rescue Nadia. I don't know what I would have done without him over the last few years. He has been there for me all the time, which makes him a rare creature, and very different from the men I was used to as a child. He is kind, gentle and supportive, exactly the sort of man any girl would marry if she had free choice. He's a wicked cook, willing to make me a meal when I am too tired to even toast a piece of bread, happy to iron and wash and to put the kids to bed.

Paul and I didn't know each other as children because he is five years younger than me, which is a big gap when you are at school but means nothing once you get older. We knew all the same people, however, and once he had left school and was socialising in the adult world, our paths started to cross more and more often at other people's homes.

By the time I met him I was starting to be able to control the black moods which I suffered when I first returned to England from Yemen and we were drawn naturally together.

We have a cosy little family house now. It stands at the end of a terrace in an area of Birmingham I know well, not far from the burned-out shell of the fish and chip shop where I was brought up.

Our house has two living rooms, a long kitchen running down to the back garden, and three bedrooms upstairs. We have a dog, a Doberman-Rottweiler cross called Saxon, who barks all day and is fiercely protective of the children. We also have a parrot who lives in the corner of the back living room. He competes with the television for the attention of the children or their cousins or their friends.

In the evenings all the children sprawl around the floor and the sofa doing their homework, bickering or clambering over the adults. If there is anything I actually want to watch on television, I have to go upstairs for some peace and quiet. It is a family home very like millions of others around every town and city in Britain, full of people and arguments and love.

If we could afford it I would like to have more animals. I would like to have a fish-tank and a couple of cats and some more dogs, but pets are as expensive to run as children if you are going to look after them properly. I'd like to have a bull mastiff and a husky and an Alsatian.

I pamper Saxon all the time and Mark, our youngest son, climbs into his bed with him. Sometimes I find them both asleep together, Saxon with his leg over the baby as if he is protecting him. I like the thought that Mark is being kept safe.

Since returning to England I have been on an English course, a childcare course, an early maths course and a car maintenance course. I was beginning to fear that I would still be taking courses and looking for things to do when I came to draw my pension. Then I heard that the local council was looking for swimming instructors.

I was always good at swimming at school and I am still haunted by a picture in my mind of a small child who drowned in a well in Yemen because he couldn't swim.

I hadn't realised how hard the exams would be or that there would be so much homework, but it is such a rewarding feeling when you see the kids let go of the sides and launch themselves off into the water for the first time.

It has been good for me physically too. The exercise has cleared my head of the cobwebs that accumulated over the years of coping with pain and worry. By the time you read this book I hope to be a qualified teacher with letters after my name, a Fellow of the Institute of Swimming Teachers and Coaches.